The Guitar's All Right as a Hobby, John

BY
KATHY BURNS

ISBN: 1494968681
ISBN 13: 9781494968687

For all the Beatle people I've met
Along the way.
And, of course, The Beatles themselves,
Without whom.....

And to Nancy for being there when I need her, which is
a lot of the time
And to Deena for her encouragement and hard work
And Brad, Mario, and Lori
For all the suggestions along the way.

... I always thought she was quite cool and I said to Sam, "Oh no, no, no, wait a minute, you're going to really miss who she was."

Maybe in the story she's got to be the strict one who has to bring John up, but what I saw of her she was a very nice woman who John loved, no doubt about it, but like any parent, any guardian would get pissed at.

But the point I'm making is I said "No Sam, you're really going to miss it" and so Mimi's character in the film is much better.

She was a fun character.

Paul McCartney
Mojo Magazine 2013

Forward

I actually met Mimi Smith in October 1973 though I had corresponded with her for at least seven years prior to that. Our paths originally crossed in October of 1966. That's when I decided to write to John Lennon's aunt for the first time. That might sound like an easy enough thing to do but it wasn't. I was a shy 15 year old Beatles fan and she was the lady who raised the man I thought was just about the greatest human being on the planet; certainly the coolest. She had recently moved south from Liverpool to Poole in Dorset, England and her new address had yet to hit all the teen oriented magazines on the newsstand. I was on my own.

It was my then new friend (and now old friend) Judy of Michigan who gave me the sacred address. Forty-seven years later I can't remember how she found it. But she had used it to write John's aunt herself and received a reply. That was good enough for me.

What follows is the 22 years that Mimi and I shared through general conversations, whether taking place through a hundred plus letters, phone calls, or all-night gossip sessions in her kitchen over tea and cigarettes. She was a fascinating woman; neither strict, intimidating nor any of the

Kathy Burns

other misleading adjectives used in books or magazines, newspapers or movies to describe her. At least not to me. After just a few minutes with her, I forgot all about her being John Lennon's aunt.

She grew up and was shaped by a world entirely different than that of her nephew or his followers but that didn't make her any less a fan. She loved him deeply, totally, and by all accounts it was returned. That others couldn't see that truly amazes me. One can't help but wonder if they even tried.

So here we go. A story of Mimi Smith through the eyes of a fan turned friend. I hope it'll bring a new understanding of the woman and her position in that special time in history. And though she would probably poo-poo any thought of there being a book on herself, I hope she might at least approve of this one.

December 2013
Minneapolis, MN

One

I grew up first and foremost a Beatles fan. Looking back I can barely remember a time when I wasn't one. Nowadays when I meet up with friends or relatives I haven't seen in years, I'm always identified as "that one who liked the Beatles". I have friends who work for the United Nations, who have played professional soccer, and were popular disc jockeys in the Twin Cities and throughout the country. But it seems my only claim to fame is being a Beatles fan. I was 13 years old when they first appeared on the Ed Sullivan Show and 14 when, on August 21, 1965, I saw them at Metropolitan Stadium in Bloomington, MN. If, by chance, you're one of those fans who wants to see every venue they ever appeared in, you'd have to go to JC Penney's in the Mall of America now to see where first base had been. The Beatles themselves appeared on stage near second base, but this is about as close as you're going to get. Anyway, I was 14 then so you can do the math.

It was the first concert I had ever been to and all these years later it still remains the best of the hundreds that followed. I can still remember arriving at Metropolitan Stadium late that Saturday morning. It had rained all night the night before and threatened to rain during the concert, but it had stopped raining that morning. At least for the time being. They weren't going to appear until 8:00 that night, but my friend Ann and I had to be there early. We had to be. It wasn't even worthy of discussion. One never knew what could happen and we couldn't miss it.

We simply walked around the stadium parking lot most of the day, trying to hear what was going on by listening to transistor radios playing in the crowd and just enjoying the ambience. My cousin and her friend had decided to come at the last minute so we talked with them as they bought the cheapest ticket at $2.75. It wasn't until late in the afternoon that things started popping. The radio stations were all (actually there were only two worth listening to back then) announcing that The Beatles had landed at the airport, only a mile or so from the stadium.

We stood on the northern side of the stadium, watching the freeway with several hundred other fans. They had to come down the freeway to get to the stadium. Two girls who didn't even have driver licenses yet were pretty sure of that.

The joke was on us. Apparently they didn't have to come down the freeway to get to the stadium. The next thing we knew the same radio stations were reporting that The Beatles were inside Met Stadium and there would soon be a press conference. Whaaa-at? How did they do that without us seeing them? (I still don't know).

The Guitar's All Right as a Hobby, John

Our next move was to run to the front of the stadium. (Yeah, like they'd walk through the front door). I turned a corner and nearly ran over Louise Harrison Caldwell, an apparent darling of WDGY, the local station that played her Beatle reports four times a day (4:10, 6:10, 8:10, and 10:10) and paid her way there.

We were young and not experienced in concert-going yet, so we simply stood by the gate we were told to wait by and…..waited. My cousin Robin and her friend suddenly walked in front of us, inside the stadium! What the…….? I think we were finally allowed in at 6:00, and dashed to our seats. We were big shots and had gone all out and paid the highest price of $5.50 for our tickets. That put us right behind the first base dug-out. It looked like a mile to the stage on second base, but we were about as close as one could get without being on the field and no one had seats on the field. As I said we weren't experienced enough to realize the distance was ridiculous.

There were two disc jockeys on stage that night; Bill Diehl from WDGY and I-can't-remember-who-to-save-my-soul-but-I-think-maybe-Charlie-Brown from KDWB and what seemed like at least a dozen opening acts but in actuality was King Curtis, Brenda Halloway, Sounds Inc. and Cannibal & the Headhunter.

One of my more vivid memories is sitting there behind first base knowing that finally The Beatles would be coming on. The disc jockeys were screwing around onstage, passing time, but nobody cared because their attention wasn't on them. We looked across the field and could see those fans in the stands in left field going absolutely crazy. Ann and I both pondered what it was they were getting so excited about.

Then the penny dropped like a brick. They were screaming at what we couldn't see. The Beatles were inside the first base dugout right in front of us! Before I could catch my breath, they were introduced and out they came. There they were. Right there. All four of them. Right in front of us; all of them waving and Paul swinging his guitar like a baseball bat (the Twins were in the World Series that year).

Yeah, it was the best. They only played 40 minutes but it was still the best. The promoter had threatened to end the concert if the screaming got out of hand (not sure what his problem was) so there was a big promotion by WDGY to not scream. I thought it had been ignored. From where I sat the screaming seemed deafening.

Apparently Louise Harrison Caldwell thought otherwise and said *"the boys"* were a bit put off by the lack of screaming. I think she was ignored as well. There were reports that the concert was ended early because crowds rushed the stage. Nope. No one rushed the stage.

When the concert did end, Ann and I ran out of the stadium and around to the side where a crowd was gathering in front of the gates that allowed a driving entry into the ball park. There was easily already several hundred people there as word traveled that the Beatles were still inside and would be leaving shortly. I don't know how we ended up in front, pressed against the large wooden gate, but there we were. Someone started screaming off to the side and suddenly we found ourselves pushed against the wood to the point that we couldn't move. The doors suddenly swung open and out came Minneapolis' finest, swinging billy clubs. I was on the receiving end of one just before we all realized there were no limousines coming out. There was nothing coming out. The

Beatles had left in a laundry truck (or was it a mail truck?) before we'd even left our seats.

The fun wasn't over just yet, though. The Minneapolis Police Chief came out in the paper several days later to proclaim The Beatles the most degenerate group of people he'd ever had to deal with, and the 16 year old girl who came out of Paul's room and said she was a fan club president was somewhat suspicious and only helped prove his point. Whatever, Chief. Forty-eight years later Paul still comes through on his tours and no one remembers your name.

⌒

*M*eanwhile, I was still feeling the rush when I returned to junior high a few weeks later and decided there had to be more to life than Robbinsdale Junior High. Seriously. So I decided I wanted to start a Beatles fan club.

I wasn't alone in my decision. There were already dozens, if not hundreds, of Beatles fan clubs throughout the country. Some of them were good, most not-so-good. That included their National Fan Club out of New York City. Though they gave away a lot of worthwhile souvenirs over the years, they were remarkably unreliable and it might be a year or better between connections. More often than not you'd receive a notice for renewal before you'd even received your first "newsletter" (which could just as well be the screenplay to A Hard Day's Night and not an actual newsletter at all). They were nothing like the well-run English Fan Club. Not even close.

I decided I wanted my club to be dependable, global, and that I would be hands-on with the members. And I wanted it to be different. How to be different? I wasn't just a Beatles fan, but a huge John Lennon fan and I wanted to incorporate that fact.

At the time Cynthia Lennon was still a bit of an enigma. I didn't know a great deal about her but I did like her and I found that a lot of people agreed. So the decision was made. It would be a Beatles Fan Club, but also integrating Cyn as much as we possibly could. That would be different from any other Beatles fan club I was aware of. It would be called The Cyn Lennon Beatle Club, but the first thing to do was to write and ask for her permission. And so I did.

It was probably a month to six weeks later when an envelope arrived, postmarked Weybridge, Surrey. Holy crap on a cracker! I knew what that meant! I opened the envelope carefully (so carefully that I still have it all these years later) and out fell a postcard-sized photograph. On the front was a black and white photo of The Beatles and on the flip side was hand written: *"Best of luck with your Cyn Lennon Club, love Cynthia & Julian Lennon".*

Hot dog! We were off and running!

I think my first move was to write a local disc jockey and get him to mention it over the radio. I even remember his name; Bobby Wayne and he was on local station KDWB. He was a KDWB Good Guy besides being a good guy and mentioned the club on the air. We received our first few members that weren't friends or family members that I had pressured to join. I remember he and I going a few rounds on the telephone over John's *"more popular than Jesus"*

remarks a year or so later, but he was still a good guy, just obstinate. And wrong.

However, it wasn't until the following summer (1966), when I wrote a letter to Datebook kissing up to them about an article they'd written while casually mentioning the fan club that the membership began to grow. After that, it wasn't only Datebook. 16 Magazine, Tiger Beat, and whatever other teenage magazines I could find also printed the club address and information and it wasn't long before we were over a hundred members and still growing. Every day brought in more and more mail. It was awesome.

Of course, I should probably note that it wasn't exactly a daring investment to be a member of the club. I hadn't wanted that either. The dues were 10¢ per month. Yep, you read that right. Only 10¢ per month. And for that they got a newsletter every other month, a membership card, a variety of photos, and a fact sheet that Cyn filled out herself. Sometimes they'd pay a year in advance and we'd get a whole $1.20 and sometimes it was every month that the little dime fell out of the envelope. It was all good.

D uring all my days (years) of wallowing in Beatledom, I'd have to say that those early years were the most congenial. It was all fresh and new and the annoying game of one-upmanship had yet to be played. It was still too early for anyone to have a story that could top anyone else. Everyone shared and helped each other and wanted nothing more than to be friends with other Beatles fans because they had something in common.

I can't tell you how many people helped promote the club and just helped in general. Some would send extra stamps. Some would help with suggestions. If I had an idea, but didn't know how to go forward with it, there was always someone in the club who knew the answer.

It wasn't long before I realized I was going to need a Vice President, as it were, to help and that's where Bunny of Ohio came in. She handled the sale of the club photos and she was a master. She not only handled the printing and sales, but she hunted far and wide for the rare photos and, if I'm not mistaken, became known to all the publications in England but especially FABULOUS 280.

It was also during this time that I became friends with Judy of Michigan. She was the President of the John Lennon Fan Club at the time and became (and still is) one of my best friends. She not only helped promote Cyn's Club through John's Club, but she was the one to give me Mimi's new address in Dorset and suggested that I write and ask her to become an honorary member.

We did have a few honorary members at the time. It wasn't that hard. George's mother was one. She would write to anyone who'd write her first so she wasn't hard to get. George's sister, Louise Harrison Caldwell (as was her name at the time) was another. She traveled the country promoting The Beatles and herself, and offered to sell us a number of photo cards she had left over from her own club. The money would go to bikes for her kids, she said. But for me, Mimi would be the real catch. I didn't know of many fans she'd written to (in fact, I think Judy was the only one I knew of at the time) and she seemed in a different class than the other Beatle parents; the one who seemed hardest to connect with.

But nothing ventured, nothing gained. I wrote her in the fall of 1966, telling her a little bit about the club, and inviting her to become an honorary member, if she so desired. This time a letter arrived stamped Bournemouth, Poole and I knew it could only be one person.

⌒

*S*he apologized for not replying sooner and went on to describe Cyn as *"a very nice girl"* and how she *"couldn't have wished for John to have a better wife"*. (I'd find out later that this was all part of the company line). She thanked me for sending her the club photographs and described one as being taken in Hamburg. But most importantly to me, she said she would be *"very pleased"* to be a member of the club and wished it every success. She was in!

The club continued to grow and now we were able to include Mimi in our list of members when fans wrote for club information. I wrote so many "thank you for your interest" letters on that old manual typewriter that I can still do it from memory. Well, most of it anyway.

⌒

*B*y 1967 we were close to 800 members from all over the United States and the world; Canada, Mexico, England, Scotland, France, Italy, Germany, Japan, Australia, New Zealand, Brazil, Peru and Hong Kong. A young girl named Pattie (not *that* Pattie, but a pen pal of Bunny's) from London wrote her own column in the newsletters and we were able to get special guest writers, i.e. disc jockeys who had traveled with The Beatles, fans who had met them, etc. to write their stories. If ever there was a question I needed answered, I'd write Tony Barrow of NEMS and have a reply by return mail. It was a good time.

*M*imi wrote the second time in January '67 to thank me for the newsletter and enclosing an autographed picture for a contest we were having. She critiqued one of the articles written by a disc jockey, saying she thought it included too many *"you knows"* but she enjoyed the read all the same, and she liked Pattie's Letter from London very much. The *"boys"* were finishing up recording an album for their next movie and she was hoping John, Cyn, and Julian would be down for a visit when it was finished.

*H*er next letter was all about the *"new record"* Strawberry Fields and Penny Lane. She explained how Strawberry Fields was a big house quite near her home in Liverpool that had been taken over by the Salvation Army for the care of little children. When John was younger they used to go to the garden parties there. They would hear the band playing and off they would go, buying all sorts of things at the stalls. Penny Lane was a shopping center and John's junior school was quite near. She seemed both surprised and proud that they had done a record about their childhood haunts.

She was quite taken with a feature on John in the December issue of Look Magazine. She even wrote to the editor saying it was the most truthful article she'd seen. They wrote back calling her Mr. Mickie Smith. Perhaps that was the beginning of her mistrust of the press.

She spoke of all the letters she'd written to fans over the years and how easy it had been when she lived in Liverpool to simply take them to the fan club office and have them stamped and sent off. She missed receiving the daily mail from those "*grand little girls*". Very often during the summer they'd come with their parents from America, Australia "*and so on*" calling on her when they were on holiday there. It eventually became just too expensive to answer all the letters. When she returned after accompanying The Beatles on their Australian/New Zealand tour, she had more than five thousand letters waiting for her. But, she said, she was in Liverpool then and answered every one of them.

She didn't talk a lot about that tour. I think most of it she spent visiting relatives in New Zealand. My impression was John invited her at the last minute and didn't allow her much time to prepare. He told her to simply throw what she needed in an overnight case and he'd buy her whatever else she wanted when they got there. She would be gone for six weeks.

I believe they went to Hong Kong first and she did go there with them. She talked of the beautiful saris that each Beatle was bringing home for their significant others. John bought the mink hat that she can be seen wearing in various pictures from the trip. She loved that mink hat and was heartbroken when she was in hospital in the 80's and someone stole it. She also mentioned how she was given instructions by John that she was never to walk through a closed door without knocking. Never! She knew precisely what he was warning her against and simply shook her head, but followed the order.

⁓

I n one of her letters that year she spoke briefly of John's sisters, simply saying they did not write pen pals. At that time, one was in France studying for finals and the other was in England but going in *"a different direction"*, neither having the time to write to fans. As odd as it might sound, in the entire 22 years that I traded letters and conversations with Mimi, that was the only time she ever talked about Julia and Jacquie to me. Though I heard about all of John's cousins and was shown pictures of them over the years, and even pictures that his sisters were in, she never mentioned their names again.

⁓

I n May she wrote that John and family had been down recently and were all very well and happy. When I stayed with her some 15 years later, she told me how strict John was with Julian, especially at meals. If he didn't behave, or refused to eat something on his plate, John would have none of it and would pick him up and put him to bed in the back bedroom. Just for the record, Mimi thought it all a bit harsh but John refused to put up with bad manners. She, of course, blamed any bad manners that Julian had on Cyn, since she was with the boy 99% of the time. Mimi said his eating habits were atrocious, all sodas and candy. Not surprising, also Cyn's fault.

Two

It was the end of August 1967 when she wrote and mentioned Brian Epstein's death. *"We are all most distressed at the sudden death of Brian. It's hard to believe. When the boys were interviewed on TV they appeared stunned. They will miss his advice and friendship."*

I knew how they felt. When I heard the news on the radio that morning, I was stunned too. It hadn't occurred to me that someone that close to The Beatles could suddenly die. It was unnerving and just a little too close for comfort.

Mimi liked Brian very much. His impeccable manners and charm won her over the first time they met. He came to the house often, she said, and assured her more than once that she should never worry about John, that he would always look after him and not let anything bad happen. That helped to ease her mind somewhat as John prepared for a career in music and not as an artist as she had hoped.

Actually the artist's life was not what she had wanted for him either. If the truth be known, she would have much preferred he became a doctor or lawyer but, she said, she knew that he was not going to follow any type of normal route while he was still at an early age. An artist was the best she could hope for.

As Brian began to fit into the inner circle, Mimi began to wonder why such a kind and generous man wasn't married. Or why he didn't have a girlfriend on his arm when he attended the parties. She finally asked Cynthia if there wasn't a woman hiding somewhere; that surely Brian wouldn't be going through life as a bachelor. It was Cyn that told her Brian was homosexual. She claims to have been completely surprised and had no idea. But that's all it had been, just a surprise. He still remained one of only a few people who attached themselves to The Beatles that she genuinely liked.

Also on that list was Derek Taylor. She enjoyed him immensely and especially loved his quick Liverpudlian sense of humor. She marveled at his large family and invited him to bring them all down to Poole for their summer holiday. They stayed in her house while she went up to Liverpool.

She seemed less impressed with Mal Evans, but in later years relied a great deal on Neil Aspinall, once he took over Apple. To her Mal was little more than a gopher, but she had met Neil when he was a young lad driving the boys around from gig to gig. Later she would telephone him when she needed to know where in the world John was or the telephone number of another member of the inner circle.

Three

1968 was one of those years where nothing really good happened. Martin Luther King Jr was shot. Robert Kennedy was shot. And John Lennon and Yoko Ono posed for a picture, dressed in white holding even whiter balloons, if that was possible.

I can still remember the first time I saw that picture and knowing in my heart of hearts that this was not some woman he was simply sponsoring in a bizarre art exhibit that included a film of bare butts. He hadn't posed with nor sponsored any budding artists before. Certainly not like this. Besides, she didn't look like a budding artist.

By summer it was apparent that Yoko was in and Cynthia was out. Letters came flooding into the club wondering what was going on and what we were going to do. After some serious thought I didn't see any way around it. We had to disband. How could you have a Cyn Lennon Beatles Club when Cyn was no longer a part of the gang? A final letter was sent out to all the members and with that it came to an end almost as quickly as it had started, just a little over two years old.

⌒

*I*t was at about the same time that one of the first Beatle fan "conventions" was held in Minneapolis. I'm not quite sure why it ended up in Minneapolis, as the two girls behind its organization, Jen and Sue, were both from Ohio and ran a club called Beatle Fans of the World Unite. But I made arrangements with a local hotel and pretty soon people from Minnesota, Ohio, California, Wisconsin, and Fridley were arriving for the weekend.

There were no such thing as videos to watch, so records were played, there was constant conversation and that first night we held a séance trying to bring back Brian. I'm not saying we did or didn't get to say hi to Eppie, but a lot of girls scattered screaming at one point (I being one of them) and we decided that was probably enough of that.

Saturday night there was a banquet held for everyone in attendance and awards were given out. By Sunday everyone was on their way home again. And what I think was the first Beatles convention came to an end with a tip of the hat to Joe Pope.

⌒

*B*ut back to Cyn's club. When it ended, Freda Kelly wrote me suggesting I contact a Sandy Schwartz in care of Apple in New York. Freda was the head of the English Fan Club and knew everything there was to know about The

Beatles. She had originally worked for Brian Epstein before being put in charge of their fan club and we had corresponded for several years. I loved Freda. She was always so kind. The US Fan Club was being renovated and this time around they were going to have State Secretaries (instead of the Area Secretaries like England) and Freda had told Sandy that I would make a good first secretary for the States.

I don't remember who wrote whom first, but shortly after I disbanded Cyn's Club, I became the Area Secretary of Minnesota and helped, as best one could from 1000 miles away, Sandy to organize. At some point we even discussed my moving to New York though that never came to be. I still had my toe in the fan club pool and that was enough for me.

⌒

My previously mentioned friends, Judy and Bunny, went to England that summer and had the good fortune to go to Kenwood and meet Cynthia (her mother let them in). I found out later that Cyn had expressed disappointment when she found out that the club had folded. She felt as if everyone was turning against her. I felt bad but still couldn't see a way around it.

⌒

With all that was going on that year, I didn't correspond with Mimi as much as we had previously. It appears my only letter from her that year was December 4th and she seemed almost apologetic about John's behavior that year.

In the world of fandom the "Yoko is wonderful if for no other reason than because John loves her" war had begun. And it would continue until long after his death. It even continues today. Never one to back away from a good argument, I was quickly labeled a "John hater" by the new President of the John Lennon Fan Club. I must have mentioned it to Mimi as she became indignant and decided that this girl was a very poor successor to Judy and was *"ridiculous and small-minded"*. Ha! So there!

⌣⟶

*M*imi claimed not to have much to say except that she was not very happy *"over recent events naturally"*. I had numerous cards from fans who didn't know John's address and she suggested that if he was lucky enough to be remembered by his fans, then I could send the cards to her and she would make sure he got them. She ended her letter by sending *"best wishes to all who still remember John kindly, or not too unkindly."* No, she was definitely not happy.

It was when we were together in later years that she described in more detail that time in history and it seemed a little more traumatic than the few words in her letter.

⌣⟶

*M*imi had never really been fond of Cynthia. She felt she had chased John throughout the years, and had purposely gotten herself pregnant in order to *"trick him"* into marrying her. But more than Cynthia, she disliked Cynthia's mother. Mrs. Powell was *"pushy"* and had to be involved in everything, according to Mimi. Even the last time we discussed the subject, she insisted that the marriage might have lasted if John and Cyn could have lived alone without her mother constantly being there. John eventually had enough and purchased a small cottage for her not far from Kenwood but Mrs. Powell insisted on spending her time at the house where she could better enjoy John's money.

Despite all that, Mimi was surprised when John came down to see her on his own and tearfully told her that Cynthia was having an affair and he was going to ask for a divorce. She felt sorry for him but wanted him to be sure before actually seeking that divorce. He was hardly out the door when she was confronted with the next bit of news. Two Virgins.

As a little aside, she never really spoke about the nefarious album except to tell me one cute story when I was there. She had gone to see The Beatles in concert and was visiting with John in his dressing room when word came that it was time for John to get ready as they'd be going on soon. That meant a change of clothes and he insisted Mimi leave while he dressed. She laughed at him and told him she'd seen him without clothes plenty of times and had even bathed him. And then she threw back her head and rolled her eyes as she looked at me. "And now, of course……" referring to the album. Yes, now, of course, we could all have stayed in the room.

I remember buying the album at a local record shop in downtown Minneapolis. I bought it on my way to work and I think I paid $5.00. At the time I worked in a rather large insurance agency that was really run by the book. Except that day. Somehow my boss, Mrs. Barrymore, found out I had bought the album and had it in a bag near my coat in the hall. It wasn't more than five minutes later that I could hear what sounded like a gaggle of geese coming from that direction. Looking, I saw Mrs. B with a handful of other old maids of the office, gawking at the album cover and roaring with laughter. She didn't fire me. At least not then. Or over that. But egads!

⌒

*P*aul McCartney, the one member of The Beatles Mimi felt closest to, started to telephone her on occasion to assure her that John was all right, while at the same time commiserating with her on the worry John was causing them both. Paul was sure it was merely a fleeting affair and Lennon would be back to his old self before long. Mimi wasn't quite so sure. In the meantime, she considered Yoko *"a thoroughly bad influence on him."*

⌒

*Y*oko Ono wasn't the only woman connected to The Beatles that Mimi felt suspect of. She had adored Jane Asher and recalled the first time Paul had introduced her. It had been at a Beatles concert. Mimi could tell he was proud of her and completely besotted. She watched as she and Jane both stood backstage watching The Beatles in concert and noted how often Paul looked over at Jane with a look of love.

Mimi felt that Paul and Jane were destined to be together forever so was quite shocked when Jane appeared on television and announced that their engagement was off. Yet she didn't connect the two, when she dropped in at the Apple Offices in London with her niece, Liela, and went into the recording studio. They watched the rehearsal for the new album, but she found the noise deafening and there was an annoying blond woman who moved about thrusting a camera in her face every time she turned around.

It wasn't until shortly thereafter when the news of Paul's marriage broke that she realized that blond photographer was now Mrs. Paul McCartney. She thought it strange that Paul hadn't made any move to introduce them when she'd been in the studio the week before. And how ironic it was that Paul had spewed his distaste for Yoko, hoping John would never marry her because at the very least she was a divorcee with a child. John, for his part, simply said Paul had finally met his match.

Four

It was a few days after Paul's wedding that John showed up unannounced. It was the first time he had been there since before the divorce and he seemed nervous and distracted as he made small talk. His looks had changed drastically and Mimi made sure to voice her disapproval.

As they walked into the sitting room, Mimi looked toward the harbor and noticed that it was Yoko Ono herself standing on the terrace. John had yet to mention his paramour so Mimi took the bull by the horns. *"Who's the monkey in the garden then, John?"*

They didn't stay long after that and there was absolutely no mention of the wedding that would take place in Gibraltar shortly thereafter. In fact, he had told Mimi that he had no intention of getting married again. I understand Hell is paved with good intentions. A lot of them John's.

A few days later Mimi received a signed copy of Grapefruit in the mail, inscribed to Mary Elizabeth Smith. She wasn't impressed and didn't know why it had been gifted.

The book remained on her book shelf for at least the next 12 years. I don't know if she ever read it.

She said she never had Yoko to the house after that but John called another of his aunts in Liverpool and asked her to have them both to dinner so Yoko could meet the rest of the family. Though Mimi wasn't there, the sisters all kept in close contact, and it wasn't long after the dinner that her sister phoned with the details.

It was like any family Sunday dinner. John was amicable. Yoko said very little. It was Yoko's apparel that caused the most discomfort. For whatever reason, she decided to dress in a see-through outfit that, Mimi said, appeared to have belonged to a French street walker. It was certainly not the way one dressed for Sunday dinner and definitely not when meeting your soon-to-be in-laws. Allegedly John went out the next day and bought her a whole new wardrobe.

⌣⟶

I don't recall Mimi mentioning seeing John after that, though they talked. She read about his wedding to Yoko like everyone else. At some point in time, his chauffeur Anthony drove to Mimi's with a car full of gold records and awards. It seems before moving from Kenwood, Cynthia had thrown out all of the various awards and Anthony couldn't bear the thought of them ending up in a dump. So he had pulled them all out of the garbage and brought them down to Mimi for safekeeping.

There were gold records hanging on the walls throughout her bungalow, and if you thought one was missing, you could probably find it in a bedroom closet with dozens of

26

others. Ivor Novella awards could be seen in the window in the sitting room. A Grammy award was on an end table. Variety Club awards were on the bookcases. And leaning up against a bedroom wall was a framed proclamation for the MBE signed by the Queen. John had traced over the signature in red ink much to Mimi's chagrin.

I asked Mimi once if she wasn't afraid of someone breaking in and stealing all those valuable artifacts. She didn't seem bothered and it was though she had never considered all those items to be of any real value. She did tell me she had been broken into once, but they'd only taken her purse. Surely the thieves had no idea whose house they were in.

Five

By the 1970's a lot of the congeniality of fandom was gone. Instead there seemed to be a race to see how many people could actually "meet" a Beatle and then brag about it in newsletters, slam books (show of hands, who remembers those?) and what came to be known as the Beatle fan grapevine. There were no computers or cell phones or iPads back then. And we couldn't wait for magazines or the latest Beatles Monthly to get our information. We had to rely on ourselves and whatever way was easiest to get the information. Besides, magazines couldn't be depended upon and The Beatles Monthly soft-soaped everything. Though we still cared about when the next album would be out, let's face it, it was their private lives that were the more interesting.

By 1972, I had moved into a small garret apartment near the University of Minnesota in an area called

Dinkytown. The group had disbanded by then and so had the National Fan Club. At any rate, I had already quit as the Minnesota Area Secretary and handed the whole mess over to Jeanne, another fan and friend I'd gone to high school with. I had resigned myself to the fact that The Beatles as a group were no more.

⁓

*D*inkytown was a fantastic area. It was populated by college kids, of which I was not. But I lived right in the middle of them and that was just about as good. One of the first things I remember is sitting on the fire escape and breathing in tear gas from a demonstration against the war that was taking place just a couple blocks away. The second thing I remember doing was going to see Magical Mystery Tour. At that time it still had not been released in the United States and if anyone saw it at all, it was a bootleg version. You had to be very careful with bootleg versions of movies or albums back then. Huge busts were going down all the time. So when I went to this showing with my friends Jean and Carole, it was understood that it was a secret location and no one was supposed to know except those with tickets. Our lips were sealed. We could be incredibly dramatic back then.

It was a hot summer afternoon when we finally found the location. I don't remember if we had to give a secret password before gaining entry, but in we went. It was a small, non-air conditioned room in a somewhat run-down building. I'm not sure what business also occupied the building. Perhaps it was best I didn't know. The room we were in was dark and dank, had a few cardboard chairs set up and an old box fan in the corner to blow the hot air and dust around. I think I chose to sit on the floor. At any rate, we weren't in there long before the film began on one of those old projectors you had in science class in high school. First class all the way.

I don't recall being blown away by the movie the first time I saw it. I think part of the problem was we were viewing a fourth or fifth generation version of the film. And it was uncomfortable in the room. The reel of film moving through the old projector was louder than the audio. All in all, I was glad to say I'd finally seen it, but I enjoyed it much better when I was able to view a legal copy.

lso during the summer of 1972, Jean and I decided to drive to Cleveland for a weekend to attend a get-together of Beatles fans in the home of a fan named Pat who ran a fan club called With A Little Help from My Friends. We left Minneapolis at 10:00 on Thursday night and got into Cleveland around 1:00 the following afternoon. The get-together lasted from Friday evening through Sunday, but Jean and I had decided we'd drive back home on Sunday morning.

Just a suggestion, but if you ever find yourself wanting to drive 900 miles at night, don't. By the time we got there, I was so exhausted I simply wanted to phone my father and ask him to come and get me. But I couldn't. We had his car.

I don't remember a whole lot about that weekend other than there was a lot of Beatle camaraderie and it was when a few of us first discussed going to England the following year. Pat, Jean, and I decided on going as did Linda, there from

New York. And even better, Linda volunteered to make all the arrangements.

⌒

*S*o in 1973 I made my first trip to England. I went on a wing and a prayer and $500 in spending money for a three week stay. It was a different time then.

We were scheduled to fly out of New York and flew into LaGuardia the day before so we could stay with Linda overnight. She had decided not to go on the trip but had made all the arrangements for us anyway, plus giving us a place to stay that night.

It was upon flying into New York that day that we first met Marie. Linda was working so Marie had drawn the short straw and won the opportunity to pick us up and take us back to Linda's place. We didn't know Marie but she had written beforehand and said she would be the one wearing a Paul button. We also found out that day that Marie would be joining us in England for our last week there.

That night, at Linda's, we met two more fans, Robin and Goldie and we all sat around talking and getting to know each other for most of the night. Goldie's name sounded so familiar to me, though I was thinking of a Gloria with the same last name. That ended up being Goldie. And, insert a chorus of *It's a Small World* here, she had been a member of Cyn's Club back in the day. Robin, Goldie, and Marie finally left for home but not until we'd made plans to get together the following morning. Linda had to work again, but Robin and Goldie offered to show us a few of the sights and Marie was coming along.

I'd never been to New York City before and thoroughly enjoyed the abbreviated sightseeing tour. We weren't in Minnesota anymore. No siree. I remember we drove by the UN Building, and were driving down one road that would eventually head into Harlem (*"just over the hill"*). Just the night before one of the girls had said the news programs didn't bother to mention the killings in Harlem because there were just too many. But we turned before reaching that point and then we were in the Village and driving by the building where John and Yoko had lived. Then it was into a Village pizza palace for lunch.

That night Linda arranged to have a limousine take us to JFK Airport and we were on our way to England.

Six

We arrived in London on early Saturday morning in late September and my most vivid memory of that arrival is when we boarded the bus to take us into London and started away from Heathrow Airport. One of the first things I saw was a McDonald's. We had left New York, hadn't we? But it didn't take long before I realized we weren't in Kansas anymore. Or Minnesota.

We stayed in a couple flats in the area of Maida Vale, and by the time we caught up on our sleep, the world became our oyster.

I loved that flat. It was decorated from the Great Depression but it had character. Pat and I stayed in the flat downstairs, while Jean, Karen, and Kathy #2 (Karen and Kathy #2 were friends of Jean's who decided to come along) had a flat upstairs. The building was owned by a Palestinian couple who lived down the block. I knew they were Palestinian because the Yom Kippur War broke out while we were there and there was a lot of excitement coming from down that block.

Our flat was deluxe in comparison to the other. We were basically one large room, with a small kitchenette and a bathroom with a shower. WITH A SHOWER!! And we had a Murphy bed! How cool is that? The others simply had a room with three twin bed tucked in there.

Once we got settled in our flats, we decided to have a quick nap before going out to look around the neighborhood. That quick nap ended up being hours and it was close to 10:00 that night when we finally got up. God bless jet lag. Someone went out to get fish and chips for us all and we decided Sunday would be soon enough to do some sight-seeing.

⟍⟍⟋

*I*t's probably no surprise that our first stop was on Cavendish Avenue in St. Johns Wood. It really wasn't that far by the tube (subway). Good deal. And we could see Abbey Road at the same time. We walked down the block and could just see the house over what seemed like 50'high gates. My God, they were big! I had my picture taken in front of them and I seemed dwarfed. That's saying something for someone over 5'8". There didn't appear to be anyone home, which was fine with me. I had yet to decide how I'd react if I actually came face-to-face with a Beatle. John was already in New York by then, so he wasn't part of that consideration.

⟍⟍⟋

*O*n our first Monday in London town we met other fans in front of Apple. We were told that Ringo usually came in every day, George very rarely, and Paul never. I wasn't particularly interested in wasting a day in hopes that Ringo *might* show up, and besides, I needed to find a post office to buy some stamps. So three of us headed off on our own, promising to meet everyone back in front of Apple later that day.

We seemed to walk forever but that's what you do in London with only $500. We stopped in Foyles Book Store, mainly because they were the people who honored John for *In His Own Write* but as long as it was a book store and I was in it, I bought Derek Taylor's new book *As Time Goes By*. I still have it and consider it one of the better written Beatle-related books I've read.

It seems to me we stopped for lunch somewhere as well, but then we were definitely in search of the post office and we found ourselves in a cute little square. *"This is Soho Square"* one of the girls who knew her way around announced. That was Kris. She was a friend of Pat's and had been there a month already. *"And there's a post office right over there."*

The post office suddenly took second place in importance. We were in Soho Square. Paul's company, MPL, was in Soho Square. And as I looked at the front of his building, I saw a large Rolls Royce parked in the small street in front of it. A Rolls? Just sitting there with the engine running?

Kris went over to the car immediately and began by asking *"are you waiting for......?"*

"No," the chauffeur answered a little too quickly. So quickly, in fact, that he hadn't waited to hear whom he might be waiting for. That was more than a little suspect.

Deciding it was no doubt Paul McCartney that the limo was waiting for because who else would it be, and figuring he would probably make an appearance soon since the car was running, we decided to wait in the park across the street. One of the deciding factors was probably the fact that while discussing our options, I leaned against one of the cars parked near us only to have an alarm go off. Oh good grief! Could anything more embarrassing happen? Ha. Oh yes. It could and did.

I was sitting on a bench, my back to MPL, trying to figure out a new camera I had purchased just for this trip. It was a Topcon 35mm. My previous camera had probably been an Instamatic. I remember deciding I wanted one that went "click" when you took a picture. The other girls stood in front of me talking between themselves when I vaguely heard Kris say quite calmly, *"there he is."*

"There who is?" But they were already out of the park and onto the sidewalk to get a better look.

I stood up and looked behind me just in time to see Paul and Linda McCartney walking arm in arm down the sidewalk and turning the corner, walking away from us. As I tried to struggle out of my camera strap to attempt to get a picture, I saw them disappearing into a door on the side of the building and my frustration became too much.

"Fuckin' A!" I yelled in complete and utter exasperation. I believe it might even have echoed. My God, he was gone and I hadn't gotten a picture! What was wrong with me?!

But he wasn't gone. Oh no. Not our kid.

He had apparently heard my outburst and backed out of the door a step and looked my way. Oh how nice. That was just great! Paul McCartney got to hear me swear like a sailor. Lovely. I prayed for the ground to open up before he came back out. Well, no, not really.

We decided we would definitely wait for him to return (he went into a store, though I'm not sure how we knew that it was a store), but we couldn't look obvious. (Yeah, like that ship hadn't already sailed). So we stood on the very same corner where he had just been and looked up at a building across the street as if admiring the architecture. That Pat was wearing a jacket full of Beatle buttons would merely be coincidence. He would never know we were waiting for him.

Keeping my eyes on the building I heard Kris, next to me, say "*Look to your right.*"

So, of course, I looked to my left. It was turning into that kind of day.

"*No. Your other right.*"

I did finally get the direction right, just in time to see Paul and Linda step in front of us. I mean, right there. In. Front. Of. Us. Maybe a foot away. Maybe not that far.

It was early afternoon and very sunny, yet he was carrying a flash light all the same. It was on and he shone it in our eyes one at a time as he walked by. "*Hello girls.......*"

Good Lord! It really was Paul McCartney! And he sounded just like him! My God in Heaven he was one good looking guy!

Someone (not me! I'd said enough already!) said something about using the flash light to break into houses, but he just kept walking. I kept thinking to myself, "*Someone say something! Someone say something!*" before he was gone forever. Then I realized I was saying it out loud and Pat was hurrying after him.

"*Paul! Paul! Would you mind if I took your picture?*"

"*No, not at all....*"

39

And that's when I was finally able to move my feet. "*Well, wait for me then!*"

We didn't get his autograph that afternoon, but we did get to take a couple pictures. As I attempted to adjust the camera manually, he looked at it and whistled. "*Ohhhhh. Topcon.*"

It might have been an impressive camera to Paul McCartney but it was a pain in the butt to me. Between it jamming on me and not knowing what I was doing with F stops and ADAs or FBIs or whatever members of the alphabet there were in the first place I was amazed I could take a picture at all. I took two of him and Linda and though the photos turned out a little dark, they were pictures and you could tell who it was so I was happy.

As he and Linda disappeared back into MPL, I collapsed onto the steps in a bundle of excited nerves. We had all but accidently bumped into Paul McCartney on the street and he had been great. Could life get any better than this? I highly doubted it.

I did what is known, or at least was in those days, as the Goldie Shuffle in Minnesota. Bill Goldsworthy was a hockey player for the Minnesota North Stars and after each goal he scored, he'd celebrate with what became known as the Goldie Shuffle, a mixture of ZZ Top and the twist. At any rate, that's what I decided to do in celebration at the exact second Linda McCartney came out of a basement exit and walked up a few steps. I froze and she smiled knowingly. She'd probably seen worse. I hoped so anyway. At least I didn't swear.

Paul followed her out and they got into the Rolls Royce that had been waiting all this time for nobody. He turned and waved out the back window. There was a reference made to the Little Rascals (Spanky, Alfalfa, and the gang, not the singing group) and "*Hiya Crabby*" (I have no idea why but I think it had something to do with the way they were waving) and then they were gone.

⟜

*W*e did finally go into the post office and then it was off to the nearest pub to calm down and rehash every single second of what had just taken place. After that it was back to Apple to see if our friends had had any luck.

They hadn't. At least not up to that point. A few more had arrived and so there was quite a little gathering by that time. We were told Ringo was inside but that was the extent of the excitement there. People seemed to be of the opinion that he would be leaving soon so we decided to wait.

There was a Ringo fan from California there, named Pattie, who was waiting near the front door of Apple. I found myself standing next to her and we began chatting. I'm usually not that extroverted but I knew her (in name only) from the Beatle grapevine, or maybe it was Cyn's Club, but she began to tell me how Ringo could be very nice but he was going through a "No Pictures" phase so it would be wise not to show my camera. I actually had no intention. Sorry, Rings.

It wasn't long before I could see the man himself coming down the hall and heading for the front. My immediate reaction was "*He looks just like Ringo*" and "*He really is rather short.*" Nothing gets by me! He came out and made a comment about "*Are you protecting the crown jewels?*" Pattie might have made a response. I had no idea what he was talking about.

The other girls were on the sidewalk and as he headed toward his car, they followed. They were actually rather respectful, I thought, and were simply calling out a few questions. And then one of them….I think it might have been Pat…took out a camera. He glared, gave them the British equivalent of the bird, got in his car, slammed the door, and off he sped.

Well! He was certainly no Paul McCartney when it came to charm.

All the girls, including the ones I had traveled with, berated him all the way home on the tube. Though I agreed with them, I couldn't help but rub it in. *"He was fine with me."*

One of them wondered why, when he looked so angry, he would give them a peace sign.

"That wasn't a peace sign, my dear."

Seven

I t was a few days later that I called Mimi and made arrangements to go down to see her. I think it was Kris who talked me into it despite the fact that I left home intending to visit her and Mimi had said to simply call and let her know what day. But suddenly I was nervous and came close to simply foregoing the visit and telling her later there just hadn't been time. But Kris had been the one who convinced me that these opportunities didn't come along every day so take advantage of it. So I swallowed my nervousness and called.

Mimi couldn't have been nicer and after giving her a brief rundown on what I'd done in London so far, we arranged for the visit to take place the following day. She insisted that I remember to catch the 'fast train'.

Everyone else seemed to have separate plans so Pat came along and we left early the next morning on the fast train, planning to spend the day.

I'd be lying if I said I wasn't still nervous because I was. I'm not sure why. She had been most inviting on the telephone the night before. But this was John Lennon's aunt I would be meeting. Probably as close as I was going to get to meeting John. After the initial greeting, what would we talk about? Would she want to spend a whole day talking Beatles? I rather doubted it.

I needn't have worried. Within a minute of entering her house I felt immediately at home. My first impressions were that she was smaller than I imagined. She was nicely dressed and there was a happy twinkle in her eyes. She didn't seem at all frail, just small. I'm guessing she was probably 5"4" or so. She looked every bit a member of the cultured class but when looking quickly around the entryway it wasn't difficult to see there was a Beatle involved here somewhere.

There was a large gold cup on a small table in the entryway, an award of some type. It seriously looked as though someone in the house had won at Wimbledon. On the wall above the silver cup hung a silver plaque stating: *"The guitar is all right as a hobby, John, but you'll never make a living at it."* I've heard that John had it made for her, but also that some fans gifted it to her. I don't know which is true, but I knew where I was when I saw it. On my second visit in 1981, it had been moved and was hanging in a place of honor over the door to a small bathroom near the kitchen.

From the entry, you could look down a hall that lead to the bedrooms and a full bath. On the hallway walls were gold records, all Beatles, no solo John. There were three bedrooms on the first floor and another upstairs. It was extremely impressive and even somewhat stately, nothing like I'd seen in London. And yet this was a holiday community and this had originally been a holiday home.

We went into the sitting room where there was a beautiful view of the harbor out the large front windows. You could walk right down to the water. It was absolutely lovely in the bright morning sun, but I can also remember her telling me how ominous it could become during storms.

She talked about John buying the house for her and how he insisted it was the most beautiful spot in the world, and if she didn't want to live there, he would. She finally agreed to it. They had looked at a number of houses, including one belonging to Richard Harris in London, but this L-shaped bungalow hidden behind trees on the harbor's edge was the one they finally chose.

As we sat down on the sofa, I couldn't help but notice there was a Grammy award on the end table next to me. There was a stereo against one wall and above it was a beautifully framed (large) black 'n white picture of John that Astrid Kirchherr had taken in Hamburg. Behind us was a wall of book cases containing dozens of books and shelves filled with more artifacts that I would check out later.

⌒

We weren't there long before we were joined by another member of the household, a large orange cat really looking the worse for wear. He came and sat in front of us, obviously curious as to who we were and what were we doing there.

The cat was named Tim and was John's, Mimi said. John had found him years before in Liverpool and when The Beatles took off, left him in Mimi's care. Tim was 21 years old, and looked every minute of it, but was still getting around and he ruled the house. Unfortunately, it wasn't long after I returned home that I received a letter from Mimi saying Tim had finally found his way to the Rainbow Bridge. I can only imagine all that he saw in his long life.

⁓

*S*he showed us where John's MBE had sat on top the television and didn't hesitate to let us know how annoyed she had been when he'd phoned and told her that someone would be down to get it from her. She found it extremely disrespectful toward the Queen, but personally I think that she enjoyed having it there to show off.

It was surreal at times being there. She would speak about John or Paul (*"And Paul was sitting on the couch right where you are…."*) and you'd forget it was John Lennon or Paul McCartney. She was Mimi, who I'd written to for seven years. There were moments when being John Lennon's aunt was almost secondary in my mind.

⁓

*M*rs. Bailey arrived later in the morning and brought us in something to drink. She was Mimi's housekeeper and had been since Mimi moved to Poole. She was an absolutely delightful woman who Mimi depended upon to keep things organized. She kept all the awards polished, Mimi said, and took special care with each one. That day she took special care of us and made delicious sandwiches for our lunch.

⟶

*M*imi talked about John as a child and teenager and how intelligent he was for his age. She mentioned how he read all the literary masterpieces, and was definitely more intelligent than the others. This story only sticks with me because she also brought out photos from Liverpool and Mendips, and when she showed me one of John's room it was littered with The Best of Mad paperbacks and magazines. I didn't say anything.

⟶

*I*t wasn't our intention to spend the night. It never entered my mind and there hadn't been an invitation offered. But the day went by so quickly, it was nearly 9:00 when I said we really should be going as certainly the trains didn't run all night.

Mimi called a cab for us and in the pitch black of night we offered our good-byes.

The Poole station seemed oddly quiet as we made our way aboard the train. We had return tickets so there was no need to have gone inside to purchase one. Even when we boarded the train we seemed to be the only ones on board. After waiting a few minutes for something to happen, and nothing did, we went back outside and found a couple conductors.

Kathy Burns

"*Oh no, the last train has already left. There won't be another until tomorrow morning.*"

What? No more trains! Now what?

We could have slept in the station, I suppose, but before we did that I thought it best to telephone Mimi, hoping she might have a better option. And she did.

"*Come back. Come back right now.*"

I don't know how long the whole episode took, but we eventually made it back to Mimi's and she found night clothes for us to use and assigned bedrooms. She gave Pat a huge room in the back of the house, complete with a sink and a space heater. I got a much smaller room that opened up onto the back patio. No sink. No space heater. But it did have a wonderful down duvet covering a down mattress. I'm not sure I've ever slept more comfortably.

*s I prepared for bed (for the record, she gave me a peignoir set that she said belonged to her niece, Liela) I could hear Mimi in the kitchen doing dishes and I thought I would ask her if there was something I could do to help.

There was nothing, she said, but pointed to a stool and told me to sit down and she'd fix us a cup of tea. And that was the beginning of our all-nighter.

The kitchen was very small. A sink, cooker, refrigerator and that was about it. I'd guess maybe three feet of floor space from one side to the other and when we sat, it was almost knee to knee. We drank gallons of tea and smoked dozens of cigarettes and talked until almost dawn. It didn't seem that anything was off-limits and I think that's the night we actually became friends.

⁓

 imi talked a lot about John, naturally; little stories that made him seem more human than anyone else had. She told me about the time he announced he was moving out and would be living with Stuart Sutcliff in a small flat near the Art College. She thought he seemed prepared for a fight, but she wished him well and waited to see how long that would last.

His return began slowly when he would start *"stopping by"* at dinner time. And would she mind doing some laundry as long as he was there. This went on for a few weeks and finally he came back, throwing his clothes down on the floor and saying that was it, he was moving back. Apparently he was unaware that electricity cost money, among other things, and when it came time to fork over his share, he had no money to give.

⁓

 hen there were the other two, George and Paul. Mimi hadn't cared for George at all when he came around for John. Forget about the way he dressed though that was bad enough, it was his horrible accent and his equally horrible use of the English language that completely turned her off. She didn't trust him any farther than she could have thrown him.

Paul, on the other hand, was quite charming but he was *"the Great I Am"* even then, she said. He never hesitated to take credit and brag about it. But he spoke lovely English and that made him okay in Mimi's book. When he would come around, she would always shout up the stairs, "Your little friend is here, John" just to take him down a peg or two. She would laugh telling me about it and I knew deep down she liked him a great deal.

There was no real opinion on Ringo. Mimi said she really didn't know him that well because he had joined the group so late. But she adored his mother and said she always made a point of looking her up whenever she was back in Liverpool.

Unfortunately, with George, she was equally critical of his family. At the time there were rumors going around that George's father was "dating" some of the fans. There's no need to mention how disapproving she was of that. Mrs. Harrison, she'd felt sorry for her when she died because she felt the poor woman couldn't help enjoying all the fame she experienced by being George's mother but she criticized her all the same. And as far as Louise, the sister, went she dismissed her completely with a wave of her hand. Mimi had no time for people who made money off The Beatles unless they were Beatles. Apparently John had told her what was going on in America with her radio shows, and fan clubs, and special appearances, and even an album. He had nothing to do with her, so neither would Mimi.

As far as Jim McCartney, she said all the parents called him Lord McCartney or Gentleman Jim because he seemed to have a royal air about him the bigger The Beatles got, but "he's all right" she laughed. When she told me this, I could picture a small yet exclusive group of "parents" gossiping about each other in a playful way. Or, in some cases, maybe not that playful.

Pattie Harrison was one of her favorites, along with Jane. Mimi said Pattie was always very nice and very pretty. So pretty, in fact, that Cynthia was jealous of her and had always tried to keep up with her fashion-wise. Mimi didn't care for Maureen at all because she was always quite rude to Ringo's mother who, as I said, was also one of Mimi's favorites.

It was all very much like any group of people bound together by ties not necessarily of their own doing. All of these people were like shirttail relatives with only one large item in common: The Beatles.

Eight

Then it was time to hear the story about John and Cyn. There didn't seem to be any hesitation when it came to telling that story. She told of the Art School days and the many times Cynthia would walk by the house in Woolton, hoping to see John while he would be upstairs hiding. She insisted Cyn had chased after him and had even asked Mimi for permission to marry him, when John was just 20 and would need a parent or guardian to sign for him. Mimi refused. When John did finally admit to her that Cynthia was pregnant and they would be marrying, Mimi gave it to him with both barrels. How could Cynthia know she was pregnant so soon? She would hardly be a month along. Where did they expect to live? How did he think he could support a family? On and on it went until John stormed out.

Mimi had no intention of attending the wedding and neither did anyone else in the family. The night before the wedding, John came to her in tears. He didn't want to get married. He was too young. He had to find a way out. But even then she had no sympathy for him. He'd laid in his bed and now he had to make it.

Mimi didn't talk too much about life after that. She said that eventually Cynthia came to live in Mendips so she wouldn't be alone. If I remember correctly, her mother was there much of the time as well. All in all, it wasn't Mimi's favorite period of time but eventually Julian was born and it wasn't long after that John moved wife and son to London.

he fans were already beginning to show up at her door by that time. If John was there, he would often times crawl out of the room so as not to be seen until Mimi scolded him for doing so and ordered him to come out and meet the fans.

She said she'd often let them in if John wasn't there and they'd usually beg for something to remember him by. She started out by cutting off the buttons of his old shirts and giving them those or cuff links perhaps. When a couple girls showed up one day in the pouring rain and thoroughly drenched, she told them to get out of their wet clothes and gave them each an old turtle neck of John's to wear while she dried their clothes. And when their clothes were dry, they were allowed to take the turtle necks with them much to their delight.

She recalled receiving a phone call one night from the local police that said there had been a call from Scotland from worried parents. Their daughters had disappeared and they were quite sure they were heading to Liverpool to see John Lennon. Had Mimi seen them? Not yet, but she would be sure to ring back if they did show up. It wasn't long before the girls arrived. They had hitchhiked the entire way just to meet John. Mimi had to tell them he wasn't there, but had them in and gave each a cup of tea while she went to phone the police back. A police car eventually showed up and the girls were given a train ticket back home.

As Beatlemania began to grow, more and more fans showed up at the door anytime of the day or night. The telephone, which was at the bottom of the stairs, rang constantly. John had suggested she move many times, but she preferred to stay in Mendips. It was her home.

And then John came home to visit one day and found her crumpled up at the bottom of the stairs. She had been hurrying downstairs to answer the phone and fell. That was it! She would have to move.

Nine

Mimi visited John and Cynthia in Weybridge on occasion though the times when John was actually home and not touring were growing few and far between. Still, she enjoyed the visits.

She told me of a time when she was there that she heard a knock on the door. No one seemed to be around so she answered it and there in front of her were two rather scraggy-looking young men. She wasn't used to the rather rougish look of the male fans. They asked for John and she told them he wasn't available then quickly sent them on their way, telling them in no uncertain terms not to return. They didn't look like the average fans, but they did look like trouble. In any event, they turned and started back down the driveway.

She'd barely shut the door when John came running down the stairs from one of the upper floors.

"Mimi! What have you done?!"

"I've told some fans to leave," she responded.

"*Those aren't fans!*" He ran out the door and down the driveway to stop the two from leaving.

It wasn't until later that he told her that was Mick Jagger and Keith Richard.

Though the best she could say about the two Rolling Stones was that Mick Jagger looked like a gargoyle, she did actually like a number of other rockers that she met along the way.

She thought Jimi Hendrix was a lovely person, very quiet and shy, but highly respectful and she liked that. Another that she found enjoyable was Stephen Stills. He talked about his mother and wanting to phone her. There could be no higher homage he could have paid in Mimi's eyes.

Mimi talked briefly about being in London at the premiere of A Hard Day's Night. All the families were there and there was a huge after-party that even Royalty attended. Princess Margaret let it be known that she wanted an autographed copy of John's In His Own Write. John refused to give her one. If she wanted a copy, she could buy it like everyone else. Mimi fretted the entire time that he would say it to the Princess' face and they'd all be spending the night in the Tower.

At the party everyone signed each other's program. Though I never saw it, she did say she still had hers and I could only shake my head at what something like that would be worth. She really had no idea of the gold mine she possessed.

*S*he did actually feel sorry for Cynthia living in the big house, more or less alone, she said. And when John wasn't touring, he'd be working in the studio and come home exhausted. Cyn, on the other hand, wanted to go out and Mimi said she would often come downstairs dressed to the nines, looking quite lovely, and hoping for an evening on the town but John would be too tired.

Mimi warned him that he had to be more attentive to his wife.

Ten

*W*e talked literally all night long. Just before finally heading off to bed she told me that when John visited, he could, of course, sleep wherever he wanted but the room she had given me was the room he usually picked and that the bed in that room had been his bed at home in Liverpool. Then, with a laugh, she said I could go home now and tell reporters that I had slept in John's bed; I wouldn't have to tell them he hadn't been there.

I also found out during our talk that she had not talked to John since he moved to New York. That was at least a year.

*I*t was just a few hours later it seemed when I got up. Pat was already up and fretting that she was going to miss a train to Liverpool that she had planned on taking in order to stay with a pen pal for a few days. And Mimi had already made us both a lovely breakfast of bacon, eggs, toast, and tea. Without a doubt it was probably the best meal I'd had since leaving the States.

*W*e arrived back in Maida Vale mid-afternoon. Pat packed her suitcase and headed back to the train station, and the rest of us sat around comparing notes on what had gone on during the past 36 hours.

It seems that a couple of the girls had decided to go back to St Johns Wood to see what might be going on there. As luck would have it, they turned the corner onto Cavendish and could see Paul and Linda coming out of the gates to get into a taxi.

The girls thought Paul was waving at them and they waved back. However, he wasn't waving a greeting, he was waving them off. *"Get off the fuckin' block!"*

All right. Nice seeing you, too.

Unfortunately these same girls were zero for two when it came to Beatles.

I think it was the following night that a call came through from Kris of the trip by MPL fame. Paul was at Air Studios on Oxford Street (finishing up Red Rose Speedway we found out later). Say no more. We were out the door and to the nearest tube station (only a block away) within record time. Minutes later we were on Oxford Street and standing in front of Air Studios.

You gotta love their subway system!

There was already a rather large group of girls hanging out. Whether they had been there all day or not, I couldn't tell you. But I hadn't been there more than 15 minutes when I could see through the glass Paul and Linda turn the corner in the lobby and head toward the front door.

I should probably explain that the people gathered there that night were divided into two groups. There were the East Coast girls on the right side and the rest of us on the left. The East Coast girls (and by no means do I mean to indict all East Coast fans, just the ones there that night) were extremely possessive. Paul was their Beatle. Too bad if we liked him, also. He was theirs and they'd prefer we kept our distance. We had very little say in the matter.

Personally, I found it all quite amusing. This second meeting with the favored one was much less stressful. No swearing. No getting tangled up in the camera strap. Seeing him again seemed the most natural thing in the world and I was quite content to watch the entire scene unfold like a scene from a…..well, from a Beatles movie.

"*He's coming! He's coming!*" This was the East Coast letting their condescending demeanor crack like a fissure in an iced lake. Yeah, they were cool all right.

The famous HE emerged with wife Linda and was immediately surrounded by the East Coast gang. I should say Paul was surrounded. Linda not so much. Both she and I were standing back for a moment and our eyes met. She smiled and rolled hers. I just smiled, hoping it didn't suddenly occur to her that I had been the girl doing the Goldie Shuffle in front of MPL just a few days before and could easily be converging on her husband if only I lived a thousand miles closer to the Atlantic Ocean.

And then they were gone. I don't know what he said to make it happen but the seas seemed to part and just like that he and Linda were walking down the block alone and turning the corner. We did walk down to the corner ourselves to see where they were going. It was to a green Rolls Royce this time, and it was his.

I read recently that he still has that Rolls and keeps it in New York.

Eleven

he next few days were spent doing the whole sightseeing thing. We traveled out to Windsor Castle and Hampton Court in our own little Magical Mystery Bus, and were driven through Henley-on-Thames simply because it was on the way home. Our tour guide was somewhat of a comedian, though I don't think he intended to be. He asked me where I was from and when I said Minnesota, he commented that he had relatives in Long Island. I informed him that was quite a ways from Minnesota; probably a good thousand miles. *"Well, that's not far in the States, is it?"* Well, it's a thousand miles. Just like here.

Another day we went through the Tower, saw the Crowned Jewels and where Anne Boylen lost her head. Best of all we went to a delightful restaurant called The Great American Disaster where you could get the best American food in town. As we sat there waiting for the best American food in town I noticed a gentlemen sitting with a little boy in a booth just across from us. I was sitting just a few feet away from David McCallum aka "Ducky" of NCIS or aka Illya Kuryakin of Man from U.N.C.L.E. fame if you're a first generation fan. I have to admit, I was just a wee bit awe-struck. I had been a big fan of U.N.C.L.E. and had taken Illya Kuryakin over Napolean Solo all day long.

⌒

At night, if we got the call, it would be back to Air Studios to watch Paul leave or we'd simply stay in, eat fish 'n chips, and watch English television. It wasn't a bad life.

Another fan from Minneapolis showed up out of no-where one day and offered to drive us all out to Henley in the little Mini she'd rented. It was a harrowing ride but we made it in one piece and parked right in front of the quaint little mansion that loomed behind the iron gates.

"He's home!" Jean, the George fan in the group, had spot-ted a limo parked in front of the mansion entrance and ran faster than a speeding bullet to the same said gate to get a better look. It wasn't much better, though. Friar Park seemed a good half mile away.

On either side of the driveway there were two lovely little cottages. Someone said that George's two brothers lived in them. I would have been quite content to live in either of those cottages. Seriously.

Despite the limo and the two guard houses, there didn't seem to be anyone around. So we decided to set out on our own and walk around the perimeter to see what we could see. Actually we couldn't see much, though at one point (that seemed miles from the house) there was a hole in the fence and beyond that was an area full of lawn sculptures.

Everyone started edging the next person on, daring them to go through the hole in the fence. I was the one who, deciding George couldn't have hit me unless he had a rocket launcher hidden in one of the 120 rooms he resided in, stepped inside the grounds. Nothing happened. Someone took a picture as proof and I was back on the outside again.

⌣⟶

I think that could have been the day Marie arrived. The same Marie who had picked us up at LaGuardia what seemed like years before. We quickly brought her up to speed on our trip so far and it was decided we would go back to Air Studios that night so she could give Paul a collection of photos she'd taken during his last English tour just a few weeks before.

The area in front of Air Studios was all abuzz that night, and there were a few more girls than usual. It didn't take long for the word to spread that this was his last night recording.

It was also extremely cold that night. Not Minnesota cold, but cold all the same. It would eventually work in our favor. But for the beginning of the evening, it was a case of everyone huddling together to keep warm, and occasionally going to the Wimpy's across the street to get a plastic cup of tea. Heaven!

It was while standing in front of Air that I was surprised by the sudden appearance of George Martin. He was leaving the building and stood for just a few seconds to adjust the collar of his coat against the cold. Everyone was very respectful and, at least within our crew, a bit awestruck. It was George Martin, who knew how to make it all happen. And he looked just like George Martin. Amazing, isn't it? That was the great thing about all the celebrities we saw that trip. They looked just like they did in the magazine photographs, except they were living and breathing and standing in front of us.

Next to appear was roadie Trevor with a box of champagne. Marie and I were standing closest to the door as he struggled to open it. It never occurred to me to help him. He suddenly turned to us as he opened the door. *"You girls want to go to a party?"*

I cannot explain to you what happened next, but both Marie and I were inside that door in a New York second. I hadn't had time to reply nor had Marie. I didn't even look at her to see what she was going to do. When I turned to look outside, there were dozens of little Beatle People faces pressed against the glass looking in. Before I could get used to the feeling of being so envied, the doorman came and told us we would have to go back outside. Say what?

"But we were invited to the party!" we protested.

It didn't matter. We might have been the envy of the girls outside but we weren't party material and back out into the nasty cold we went.

I think Trevor was sacked not too long after that. Something to do with missing tapes and bootlegs if I remember correctly.

At any rate, it ended up being a long evening; much longer than I had ever waited before. The doorman who had kicked us out earlier seemed to have a turn of heart. Eventually he let us all in to warm up, but we had to stay in the lobby, no trying to sneak upstairs or we'd be out on the street again.

I was standing against the lobby wall, simply enjoying the warmth, when I saw the floors light up on the elevator.

Someone was coming down but we didn't know who. It could be Paul but then again it could be the cleaning lady.

As the elevator continued its descent the sound of someone singing could be heard. It was mid-October but they were singing Christmas carols. And though the songs were out of season, and perhaps a little out of tune, there was no mistaking that voice.

Suddenly, as the elevator door opened, all of the girls turned and fled outside. What was this? Would he be angry that we were there and that's why they'd hurried out? There were only the dumb ones not from the East Coast left inside and I, for one, wasn't moving. It was just too damn cold out there. I was willing to take my chances.

Paul walked out of the lift with Linda, whistling now. As they headed across the lobby he looked directly at me.

"Are you here for the job interview?"

Huh? It seemed a ridiculous question to be asking at any time but especially then. But I didn't care.

"Um, yeah." I didn't know what else to say. I had no idea what the job was, but I was game.

He only laughed and kept walking. By then I was fairly certain there wasn't much champagne left and knew who drank it. The subject of a job interview was dropped.

We followed them outside where, once again, he was surrounded by girls, but more this time. Marie hurried to pull her pictures out of her bag and tried to gain his attention

"Paul, I've got some pictures for you….."

He looked back at her while pushing through the crowd. *"Next time…. Next time!"* he finally offered.

Marie is a little Irish spitfire and that's all it took. She hadn't waited all night in the cold to be rebuffed like that.

Without any warning the pictures flew up in the air going in all directions. "*Fuck next time!*" she yelled back.

Whoa!! She was worse than me! Once I was sure no lightning bolt was going to strike us down, I was nearly on my knees I was laughing so hard. Paul kept walking but it was pretty obvious he'd heard her. I think he might even have cringed in fear a little.

It wasn't more than a couple minutes before the green Rolls came around the corner. Denny Laine had somehow left the building unseen to join them and he was driving. The car circled the block twice, both times Paul waving frantically while Denny honked the horn. But all the girls had decided he deserved to be punished and had chosen to turn their backs, ignoring him. Me? I was still laughing.

Beatle fans. You've gotta love 'em!

Twelve

Those three weeks seemed to fly by. The Minnesota contingency left first. Both Pat and Marie stayed behind for another week. I was looking forward to getting home but knew I was going to miss England as well. I had hoped to talk to Mimi one more time before leaving, but when I phoned Mrs. Bailey had answered and said she'd been called back to Liverpool as one of her sisters had taken ill.

Once home again, the mundane set in. It was back to work with very little to look forward to. I did talk to Marie, Robin and Goldie from time to time and by the end of the year they were telling some rather interesting news.

They would go to see John arrive at the recording studio in New York as often as they could and he began to refer to them as 'The Greeting Committee'. They eventually had tee shirts made up with 'The Greeting Committee' printed across the front, and gave one to John. The next time they saw him he was wearing the shirt and showed it off proudly. They were naturally excited but not as excited as what they were beginning to figure out.

When they first started going to the studio, it was John, Yoko, and an assistant that would arrive. And then, as the encounters grew in number, it was suddenly John and his assistant and no Yoko to be seen. John and Yoko were always together, they explained excitedly. If they weren't together then….that had to mean they weren't together.

It wasn't long before they'd discovered through the grapevine that John and Yoko had separated and John was now with his assistant, May Pang.

I immediately wrote Mimi of the news. "*If your news re: Y. is sound, well that'll please me I can tell you. It's his only hope of getting on an even keel again,*" she responded.

Someone had sent her recently taken pictures of John and they made her sad. She thought he looked lost somehow and might be wishing The Beatles would get back together. It was those times she thought he missed all the happy times the group had together. He began phoning her again and had told her that Paul was coming over and that he would be seeing him. She hoped that happier times would come out of their meeting.

She was surprised to hear Julian had been there. John seemed really pleased to have him, and said he thought Julian was pleased to be there. Mimi was also surprised to hear Cyn had taken him over and stayed the two weeks, but she could also understand Cyn wanting to keep an eye on Julian. Very little was said about that trip other than that. At least at the time.

Meanwhile, back in Dinkytown, things were still traveling along the road of the mundane until I received a phone call from a disc jockey friend of mine. His name was Rob Sherwood and the radio station (U-100) was hosting a telethon for St. Jude's Hospital. They were going to broadcast from a local shopping mall and he wondered if I could get John Lennon to appear. Oh, John Lennon? Just John? No one else? Why not all The Beatles?! Yeah, let me get right on that. He did a lot of fast talking and I was still doubtful. For starters, I had no idea how to get in contact with John Lennon. *"Call his aunt."*

So I did.

Mimi was very kind. She gave me his address at a New York hotel and advised me on how to go about asking him to attend. *"He's terribly soft hearted, tough reporters make him sarcastic. A soft word and he's finished. Lay it on."* She was sure he would do it if he could, but also warned me that he might not even receive the letter. Some of hers had disappeared.

Well, I gave it that old college try. I was given stationary from the radio station, and wrote as if I was employed by them. It was a lovely letter if I say so myself. But there was no reply. John Lennon would not be appearing at the St. Jude Telethon. Perhaps they could find someone who knew Elton John's aunt.

*M*imi seemed to hear from John on a somewhat regular basis again while he was separated from Yoko. If he didn't phone, he wrote and she was always pleased when she heard from him. He seemed much more like his old self, she thought, and she had continued hopes that he and Paul might get back together again.

Despite the phone calls and letters, it was on the news that she heard about the incident at the Troubadour in Los Angeles. She was most incensed about the photographer outside the club that claimed John had hit her and was going to sue. Mimi didn't have a great deal of love for reporters, except for a few in Liverpool, and was sure if he had hit her, she had it coming. Eventually the law suit was dropped. Mimi was delighted but wished he would just come home.

⟨⟩

*H*e wanted her to come over for Christmas at the end of 1974 but she had been ill and had no desire to go. Eventually he tried to talk her into moving to New York. He told her he was looking to buy a house so when she came she'd have some place to stay instead of a hotel. But I don't think she ever gave it serious consideration. She was too old, she told me, and what would she do in New York on her own? The rest of her family was in England and she was quite content to putter around in her own home. Once Yoko returned to the scene, the subject was never brought up again.

⟨⟩

*B*efore all that though, Mimi was surprised to receive a telephone call from Yoko. She was in London at the time and seemed frantic to see Mimi right away. Afraid that something might be wrong with John and preferring not to have her come down to Poole, Mimi offered to travel to London and meet her at her hotel.

Once at the hotel, Mimi told me she actually felt sorry for Yoko Ono. Yoko was occupying an entire floor and, according to Mimi, she seemed very small and lonely as she directed the people around her and played the role of millionaire Empress.

Mimi said the most she got out of the trip was a free night in a luxury hotel. She wasn't entirely sure why she received the panicked phone call. There didn't seem to be anything wrong with John, and certainly nothing to be in a panic over. In fact, Yoko told her he had called several times while she was there, though Mimi rather doubted it. She was certain he would have asked to speak to her if he'd known she was there. The most she could surmise from the trip was that Yoko wanted her to convince John to return to her.

I'm not sure what Mimi told Yoko but she didn't call John and certainly didn't try to convince him of anything. Getting him to return to Yoko would have been the last thing she would have requested of him. If future reports are to be believed, that job was turned over to Paul McCartney.

It wasn't long after that John was "allowed" to return, as the rest of the world rolled its eyes. Mimi wasn't thrilled with the news but as long as John kept in contact, she accepted whatever turns his life took.

Thirteen

I was not alone in visiting Mimi. From time to time she would talk about other fans coming to the door and there was a small circle of friends who visited regularly. Marie visited every time she went to England. Bunny and Judy, together and alone, visited several times. Then there was the odd (no pun intended) fan who had Harbour's Edge as part of their pilgrimage. She was surprised when she found out one of her doctors was a Lennon fan or that a fan who had shown up recently was a school headmaster. In her totally biased way she found that the John fans were by far the more intelligent.

The fans who seemed to puzzle her the most, however, were those who organized the various Beatles conventions and the dealers that made a living off of Beatlemania. She found it all rather distasteful, but at the same time she was interested in who was there and any gossip I could find.

She spoke of a visit by two German "*fanatics*" who ran a club called Beatles International. She felt sorry for them because after traveling 6 ½ hours to get to Friar Park, two dogs were set upon them. Mimi found that most unkind so she invited them in. *"Altho they spoke English quite well, by the end I was exhausted."* They later met with disfavor when they published a picture and article about their visit without her permission.

But all in all, she enjoyed the fans; especially the Americans. *"If Beatles have done nothing else, they got me knowing the young people of America, and that for me has been good."*

⟨⟩

During one of her visits in 1974, Marie and Mimi made a cassette tape for me. It was almost entirely Mimi actually, taking over the microphone after Marie had gone to bed. She talked about anything and everything on that 90 minute tape. Or was it 60? At any rate, I remember listening to it again after John died, and for the first time felt chills run up my spine as she talked about John and the occasional trouble he got into in the States. She told him that he'd better watch himself and what he said *"or someone will shoot you sure as heck."* I didn't remember hearing that on any previous listens.

⟨⟩

There was a time in the 70's when May Pang came down to visit with, according to Mimi, Ringo's secretary. When May had written to ask if she might come down, Mimi panicked and called John. Was there a reason she was coming down? Should she have told her no? *"Just treat her nice"* John told her. As far as I know they had a lovely visit.

*S*everal times over the years she invited Judy and I to both visit at the same time. And at one point we thought seriously about it. Mimi was so excited. She was going to paint the inside of the house and make sure Mrs. Bailey would have everything ready.

She casually mentioned in one letter that she hoped we wouldn't mind but John, Yoko and the baby said they would be visiting about the same time. We were not to worry, though. They could stay at a hotel.

We did, however, worry and though our plans hadn't been anywhere close to finalized, we decided then might not be the best time for our visit. I, for one, had no intention of sitting in that living room overlooking the harbor while John and family stayed in a hotel. Nor did I really fancy being there when he met with his aunt for the first time in years.

Mimi might have been right for he never showed. There was some excuse about having to leave Japan and return to the States immediately to sign some papers. She wasn't really sure what it was about but in the end said she thought it would have been too much commotion for her anyway. There were several more times during the years when he would promise her they were coming and there was always a reason that kept him from doing so. The stars weren't aligned right. The moon was off. Who knows? He always seemed to make it as far as Japan though. He would send a gift of some sort to appease her until the next time but all she really wanted was to see him.

Fourteen

*M*imi wrote me the night Sean was born. "*I was fast asleep when the phone rang. John – (who else at all hours) to tell me about the birth of his son......He phoned from the New York hospital. I gather he's living there until they depart for home. I've been instructed to phone every day, direct line to their rooms. He's beside himself, giving every detail of weight, looks, it's lovely, it's beautiful, it's like him except the eyes, taken dozens of photographs already and so on – so what!*" and later in the letter, continued a few days later: "*The 'great event' was practically ignored here, except for a few lines in one or two papers. They will be home now. I'm wondering what difference it will make. I can't see anything 'motherly' in 'MRS'. Oh well....*"

She really was on a roll that night. Paul, Ringo, George, Cyn; no one was left unscathed in that letter!

Discussing one of the fans and Paul: "*Well, I just lose patience with such reckless stupidity. There must be reason in all things and to chase round after an aging Romeo, and worse still getting into debt to do it beats me. It would not mean a thing to him even if he knew, apart from boosting his ego, which doesn't need any help and for Heaven's sake,*" *why he does these tours I can't think. Only, of course, he may miss the publicity, which he loves. I say you can't go back trying to recapture the careless rapture of youth, etc. etc. It could never be the same as it was when they were at their peak, the four of them. It's nearly 12 years since L'Pool first went mad on them and then America. John may at some time feel like doing the same but I hope he won't."*

And Ringo: *"I hear Ringo has announced his final departure from this country to live in America. Announced if you please. I don't care either way. Certainly no announcement is needed. – Just go and remember where you or he got his chance, with a big slice of luck thrown in. Really such arrogance. A little less bravado would be appreciated. 3 children left behind. Financially they'll be all right, but that's not everything. I don't hear anything but gather his and George's divorces are through. I'll try and see Ringo's mother next time I go North and get all the news. I know she'll be upset. Announcement indeed! It annoyed me."*

George: *"As for George and all that Harri Krishner or whatever they call themselves. I couldn't blame Patty if she had to put up with that lot. Those screeching Jennies wandering all over the house with their silly nonsense, banging tambourines and wailing all day long. Money does go towards softening of the head, altho between me and you, I wouldn't mind the money and keep two feet on the ground."*

And finally Cyn. She'd received a letter from a fan who had been visiting Cyn. *"Well, she [the fan] indicated that Cyn didn't want her address known. [She] knew but couldn't tell me as, more or less, it was private. It irritated me. There's no need for anyone connected with The Beatles to hide; one never hears of them, only an occasional mention. So she is quite safe. What an irritating letter to write. She could see Cyn had had her share of worry, etc. And [she] feels so bad that I don't see Julian and no wonder Cyn wants seclusion in this world. Really such rubbish! It's entirely Cyn's own fault. Seclusion! Bah!"*

It was somewhat presumptuous of the fan actually. If Mimi had truly wanted Cynthia's address, she could have had it in five minutes.

But as I said, she was on a roll that night.

I'd be remiss if I didn't mention that she eventually grew to adore Sean, and she loved Paul. The others? Well.......

⟨~⟩

When the next letter came about a month later (November 9, '75) Mimi was still wound up over the fan who has visited Cyn and what she'd said in her letter about Cyn suffering so and needing privacy from the fans.

"Fans are no problem. It's no use pretending to hide from fans who are not there, apart it seems from [she named two fans devoted to Cyn]. *As far as keeping the address secret. Such rubbish, did you ever......As far as the new protector* [this would be John Twist], *his duties will be light. I've heard several times about men just passing by – and falling in love on sight, hardly a word spoken! That's it – great stuff. Matter of fact I'm highly suspicious of these gallants who step forward so willingly to protect a twice divorced woman aged 36 – with money, unless of course we've got another Elizabeth Taylor. The mother used to say, also,* [that] *men were chasing her. They were the lucky men who couldn't catch up, believe me. If it's true. But I never believed her stories*

"My sister says I should thank the girl for sending the photographs. I may but I might be rude if I did it now. These 'in-the-know people' are annoying..........

My sister Anne phoned and I told her about another prospective lover and protector. She let out a yell and said 'Not another!' All in their mind says she. Anne says they hope all this 'protector' business gets to my ears. My God, Kathy, [Cyn and her mother] *tried hard to get rid of me.*

I just said nothing and let them get on with it, knowing their reign would be short. I think he knows. He's always telling me he loves me, even if he isn't in constant touch, but always thinking of me. And — I'm still here. I've never hung on him. I love John, of course I do, but really the 4 of them [The Beatles] have been a pain in the neck at different times."

Poor Mimi. Cynthia would continue to be a thorn in her side for probably the rest of her life.

Fifteen

While Cyn was busying herself with her next husband, Paul McCartney was making plans to do a concert in St. Paul in June of 1976 and I was intending to go.

When I think back on those days, I could laugh. It was $9 to see Wings and it was general admittance. I remember telling my friends he'd better be good for $9! After all, I'd seen all four Beatles and only paid $5.50. I still use that argument when I see what is being charged for concert tickets today. *"Are you serious? I only paid $5.50 to see The Beatles. The Beatles, for cryin' out loud!"*

I got off work at noon that day and was sicker than a dog. I don't know why. Maybe it was the excitement. Maybe it was something I ate. Maybe it was the $9 investment, but when one of my friends called to say we were going to meet his plane at the airport, I was suddenly a whole lot better.

Becki (one of the girls attending) said she heard on the radio that his plane would be landing at Bierman Field instead of the International Airport. That would have been all well and good because it was within walking distance of my apartment. But it was also a football field so chances of him landing there were really pretty slim. So we tried the International Airport. We covered the gold concourse, the green concourse, the blue one, pink, yellow, polka dot…. whatever concourse we could find, we covered it. Nothing. If I remember correctly, someone called someone and found out he was landing at Holman Field, a small airport in St. Paul. So off we went.

We were somewhat heartened to see other Beatle fans already there. This must be the place, we figured, as we planted ourselves and waited. And waited. And waited. Once an actual plane did land but there wasn't a Beatle aboard. Finally we decided it was getting late and if we wanted to get a decent seat with the general admission, we'd better head to the Civic Center before the doors opened. Fortunately the arena wasn't far at all.

Once there, it was another game of waiting. This time for the doors to open. Word eventually started to circulate that he had just landed at the International Airport. Figures.

I'm always amazed when you seem to be the first one in front of the door, it opens and by the time you get down to the arena, the first 15 rows are already full. How do they do that? I stood there like a dummy looking around for someone who'd tell me where to sit when Jean pointed out the seats in the balcony behind the stage. She'd already seen him in Detroit just a few days prior and said that would be a great place to sit. AND…..it was still almost empty.

By the time we got up there, we could have second row yet it was so close to the piano on stage that it felt like you could reach out and touch it. Not bad. Not bad at all. I was happy.

There was a young girl sitting in front of me. She was saving several seats for friends who hadn't yet arrived and was full of enthusiasm. She loved Paul and couldn't believe she was seeing him, she explained excitedly. She had a bouquet of fresh flowers and wondered if I thought it would be silly to try and give him the flowers when he came over to the piano. Nope, not at all. Give it a try, kid. Then she changed her mind and thought it might be cooler if we all threw a flower at him when he came to the piano. That sounded good too.

And somewhere there is a home movie of flowers raining down on one Paul McCartney as he approached his piano in St. Paul, Minnesota. And after all the flowers had floated down, one last one suddenly appeared and he clawed at it, trying to catch it. It came down all on its own because the person who held that flower got too excited seeing him and forgot to throw it. But at least she didn't scream a profanity.

We were inside the Civic Center a good two hours before the concert started. More waiting. But there was almost a giddy excitement running through the building. For the vast majority of people there, this was their first time seeing Paul. Most of them had been too young to see The Beatles when they had been in Minneapolis in 1965. Our little group sat quietly surveying the crowd. From where we sat we could see friends sitting in the front row right in front of the stage. How do they do that? And we could easily read some of the signs.

At 8:00 I asked Jean (the one who had seen him in Detroit) if he had started on time there. And would I have time to run to the bathroom. *"Sure, go ahead,"* she replied and as if it was a signal to the technicians, the lights suddenly dimmed. I could hold it.

The stage was completely dark but we were able to see people moving around and a roar went up from the crowd.

> *Sitting in the stand of the sports arena*
> *Waiting for the show to begin*
> *Red Lights, Green Lights, Strawberry Wine,*

A red light, then a green light and then he was there. Oh yeah, this was going to be worth every penny of the $9. I would've paid $10! Maybe even more!

Thirty seven years later, I can still remember odd little bits and pieces of that night. Paul spent a lot of time on the piano. And he was close; really close to those of us in the balcony. He seemed to know exactly where Jean's movie camera was and spent a good portion of his time looking into it. But beside the camera, he seemed to develop a certain affinity with the balcony that we didn't mind at all. We were also very close to the smoke bombs used during Live and Let Die. The first two rows of the balcony were engulfed in smoke and so was the guy on the piano. Nice touch.

It was during Silly Love Songs, then his latest single, that the crowd below us suddenly surged forward from the back of the ground floor and we lost sight of our friends who'd been sitting in the front row. But it was an incredible sight to watch. Later we were told it had all been planned and they allowed the people forward at the same time every night. Well, be that as it may, it was still an exciting moment.

I'm not sure how we got out of the Center that night but suddenly we were outside on an upper level. We were able to look down at the drive-in entrance to the building where a large black limo was parked. It didn't take anyone very long to figure out who that was waiting for.

That area was thick with people as they waited for Paul to come out, everyone discussing the concert they'd just seen and its highlights, but as the minutes passed the people started to disperse. It was getting late and he still hadn't emerged. Word spread that they were inside receiving awards from the record company. I guess we were grateful that he was still inside. But come on, already. He had to leave sometime.

Nor am I sure how long we waited out there, looking down at the limo, but it had to be over an hour. Probably longer. (I didn't think I'd mention this part to Mimi). Finally..... FINALLY....they came out. There were probably 50 of us left as he looked up and waved. I remember thinking how impressed he would have been with the number waiting if he'd come out right away.

The limo started up the long driveway and we ran ahead so we could catch up to it on the street. As we turned at the side of the building, we were confronted by hundreds of people who had been waiting there. Those who had left the area where we had been, had simply gone in front to wait. It didn't look like a single person had left.

We ran right beside his car as it headed slowly toward the freeway. Paul was sitting on our side of his car, laughing and waving at those of us running beside him and, of course, giving the thumbs up. We simply applauded as we ran. It had been such a great show and such a great night. Except for his concert in Ames, Iowa in 1990, I don't think I've enjoyed him more.

Sixteen

hough there were many members in John's family, I heard regularly about John's cousins David and Michael. Both their jobs allowed them to stay with Mimi at different times and by all accounts she enjoyed them both immensely. So much so that John would often sound jealous when she talked about them to him, calling them her "*favorites*".

I talked to both David and Michael at various times when I would telephone and they'd answer. They were always extremely gracious. And Michael once was kind enough to write to let me know that Mimi wasn't well and had gone to stay with another cousin, Liela, since she was a doctor.

Mimi bragged a lot about Michael, David, and Liela. David and Liela were brother and sister and belonged to Harriet. Michael belonged to Anne. Liela was a "*clever doctor*", while Michael worked for a bank and David for a petroleum company. I'm sure they were actually higher-ups, though she never got terribly detailed. I know that she simply enjoyed their company and the three seemed to keep a protective eye on her.

There was another cousin, Stanley, who lived up in Scotland (belonging to Elizabeth/Mater). I had no idea he even existed until I was staying with Mimi in 1981 and she brought out a box of photographs, and there he was. If I'm not mistaken she said he was an automobile salesman.

Of the Stanley sisters, the only one I spoke with was Anne. Mimi stayed with her numerous times and I would call on occasion when she was with her right after John died. Harriet and Elizabeth both died while we were corresponding, and, of course, Julia years before.

⌒

I find it interesting that the members of the family who speak out the most now, are two I heard virtually nothing about in all the time I knew Mimi. And that they waited until after Mimi was gone before coming forward. Not that there's anything wrong with that. I didn't decide until Mimi was gone to write this book, after all. Her *"favorites"* are rarely quoted if at all these days.

I'm not sure what all that means, but I'm sure it means something.

⌒

*A*fter John's death another character appeared and I asked her one day about Charlie Lennon. I had never heard of him before, which of course meant nothing, but I wondered if she had.

The Guitar's All Right as a Hobby, John

"*Yes! This Charlie Lennon is another who has crawled out of the woodwork. This is the 2ⁿᵈ time I've heard of him. Once from the L'Pool Fan Club (the John Lennon Club) asking if I knew him as he claimed to know me well. He may be a relative of the Lennons for all I know but honestly, Kathy, I've never seen or heard of him either, for I was with John from his birth. I'm sure I would know and do know. That is the truth. I heard from the fan club that he was talking about John and me, and getting free beer on the strength of it. Another miserable thing trying to trade on the name.*

"*....A couple of years ago a man from America appeared here, claiming he was a distant relative of John's. His great, great, great Grandfather was a Lennon – from Liverpool, of course, and what with telling who had married who, my aunt this, my great cousin that, I was getting bewildered. He had written out a family tree. I just could not see the point of coming to me with all this rigamarole. I was jolly glad Michael was here. Finally we got rid of him and I've never heard of him since....*

"*...this Charlie Lennon person, he seems a poor thing, but I certainly know nothing about him. Neither did John. I wish you would tell anyone else who may ask you. I do get tired of these people, press, TV, etc. and long lost relatives. The name Lennon has a strange effect!*"

From an October 1986 letter, continuing on the subject:

"*Yoko phoned last night asking me about this Charlie Lennon. Another scrounger like his brother I've told her. I have never seen or heard of him in my life. Neither had John. It's strange the people appearing when John is dead. Where were they when he was alive?*"

Indeed.

Seventeen

John Lennon said "weren't the 70's a drag?" And he was right. Oh there were moments, of course; the trip to England, the Wings concert. But the latter part of the decade really lacked for any type of real excitement in the Beatle arena. They were busy suing each other and my interest of who was going to be declared the 'winner' was minimal at that point. Just get it over with!

So I settled for something new. I went to my first Beatlefest. This was, of course, back when they were still allowed to call it Beatlefest and you went to see the videos because videos had yet to be a mass-produced item with their own shop. There was the occasional interesting guest and the Dealer Room which offered every Beatle item ever made; though not for the original price. Yoko hadn't yet started to call the shots so pretty much anything was up for sale and dealers were still allowed to sell items that Mark Lapidos sold.

My first Beatlefest was in New York City. I was invited to attend with my friend Barb who was going as a dealer. It was massive! The Dealer Room, that is. I tried to get around to see what was being offered, but it was so crowded and Barb was so busy, that I spent the majority of the time behind the table helping her.

I do have a few memories of that weekend, though.

After we arrived and checked in to our hotel, we decided to take a cab to the Dakota. Barb had been there before on previous 'Fest trips, but that would be my first time and I was eager to go. As I said, we took a cab and less than 5 minutes after arriving, here came another cab carrying three of Barb's dealer friends. It seemed that everyone had the same idea that afternoon.

There really isn't much to do there aside from looking up at the building and wondering if John was up there and if he was, what was he doing? Maybe gazing out his window, looking at us looking for him? There was the slim possibility that he might venture out at the exact moment we were there, but I wasn't holding my breath. Still, if he did emerge, I'd already decided I wouldn't be able to approach him nor would I have anything worth saying that he would want to hear. There were only two people in the world that I felt unworthy of; John Lennon and Bob Dylan. They were way out of my league intelligence-wise and every other kind of wise. Mimi told me I should never have felt that way around John. And maybe she was right. I'd never have the opportunity to find out.

I did, however, have the opportunity with Dylan several years later. I worked in an auto dealership at the time that also sold RV's. One afternoon one of the girls who worked with me, found me on the computer in what we called The Computer Room back in those days. The computers were that big. Her voice was shaking.

"Dylan's here."

"Dylan who?"

"Bob Dylan. He's out back looking at RVs."

It was the hidden excitement in her voice. I knew she was telling the truth. Screw the computer. Screw work. I had to check this out.

I headed into the waiting room where a larger than normal group of employees stood around talking. They were talking about what I'd come to check out. *"Where is he?"* I asked no one in particular.

"Out back in the RVs" came a voice from within the pack.

"Who?" The finance manager had been sitting on the couch watching television when the circus suddenly came to town. *"Tell me who it is,"* he continued, *"and I'll take you back there in the golf cart."*

I could have driven the golf cart myself. I'd done it before when I'd had to track someone down in the back 40. But letting Ralph maneuver the cart allowed me to concentrate on what was going on and what was coming next.

We rode back into the sea of RV's and were about 50 feet away when I was completely aware of who it was and what we were doing.

"Do you want to stop for an autograph" asked the obliging finance manager.

"No!" Oh God, no. *"Just keep going. Make it look like we're looking at RVs too."*

And he did, bless his heart. We went right by Dylan, close enough that I could have touched him. Close enough that I could hear him say *"Meetcha back on the show floor,"* in his best *Subterranean Homesick Blues* voice. However, it was not said to me.

We did a U turn and went back to the waiting room. Employees still mingled around, but the majority of them were now in the service department, looking out the side door and waiting for Mr. Tambourine Man to go by.

I made my way to the cashier area and was talking to the receptionist about the best day ever at work when the salesman who had been helping Dylan suddenly appeared. He was not my favorite human being so it only figured he'd be the one Bob would pick out.

"Whatever you do," he sniveled, *"don't make a scene. He doesn't like scenes."*

I gave the dolt my best stink eye. *"I don't make scenes,"* I muttered.

"Well, make sure you don't. He hates being recognized."

He was a major eye roll type of guy so I gave it to him. He had shown Bob Dylan a motor home and now he thought he was the President of his fan club and in charge of his security. Back off, moron.

While there he asked for the bill that was Dylan's and laid down an American Express card. There, on the card, it said Robert Zimmerman dba Bob Dylan. He didn't like being recognized but made sure both names were on his credit card. And don't leave home without it.

Mr. Dylan never made it into the show room. Word had it that one of the less educated employees walked up to him and asked if he was really Bob Dylan and that sent him back to his car instead, where he waited for his brother to take care of business and then drive him home.

I never saw Dylan again though I was in a local grocery store when one of the stock boys hurried up to the cashier I was doing business with and breathlessly told her that Dylan was back in the frozen foods.

I've driven by his house out in the country several times as well, but never drove in and knocked on the door. Knock, knock, knocking on……..Nope. Still intimidated.

For the record, Mimi blamed Bob Dylan for introducing drugs to the young Beatles. I wasn't sure he was the one, but she wouldn't hear differently. It had been Bob Dylan and she didn't care if he was my neighbor. She would never forgive him for turning The Beatles on.

*S*o I digressed a little. Sue me. Now back to the Dakota and deciding I would never have the nerve to approach John.

There wasn't an opportunity. We had stood there barely 10 minutes, talking amongst ourselves, before the doorman came up and told us we would have to move along. And we did. Like good little Beatles fans we obeyed. And only a few months later we would wonder aloud why we were told to move along while the demon bastard from Hawaii was allowed to stand there all night. I'm still wondering.

I wasn't able to see whoever the special guests were at that particular Beatlefest. Marie had shown up and I had a much better time talking at the table. It wasn't as if I didn't see anyone noteworthy that weekend though.

Right outside the dealer's room on Saturday afternoon there was suddenly a loud banging noise. A consistent banging noise. An annoying consistent banging noise. We looked out the door to see who it was. To me it looked like a homeless person beating a drum in a monotonous rhythm while chanting God knows what. Marie groaned. She knew who it was. "*Who? Who?*"

"*It's David Peel.*"

David Peel? The fellow who followed John Lennon around clutching his leg and got him to help produce an album? That David Peel? Oh God.

"*Please tell me John's no longer hanging with this guy.*"

"*John dropped him like a hot potato.*"

Good.

⌒

The New York Beatlefest was followed by a couple of conventions held in the Twin Cities that Barb put together. The first one was great fun. It was held in the late great Leamington Hotel in downtown Minneapolis and judging by the attendance of both fans and the dealers, it seemed to be a success. Marie was the special guest with a fantastic slide show of her trips to England and McCartney encounters and everything seemed to go smoothly.

The second convention was held the following year at the University of Minnesota. It was a venue that would attract a lot of people, but didn't have the intimacy of the first one. There were other chiefs involved as well and it was run too much like a business with people running around with clip boards barking orders and making sure you were where you were supposed to be at any given moment.

Still, the ever famous Louise Harrison, sister of the far more famous George Harrison, was also a special guest and arrived with her daughter Leslie (an extra mouth to feed as it were but hey, Louise was the self-proclaimed "mum" to all the fans so what's a few more dollars among family.) It was at that time that Louise hadn't spoken to George in years but she still managed to take the stage and give her standard talk. Somehow she found something to say. And later that night a few of us ended up in her room where she showed us her photo album from a recent trip to England. George had not been there so her other brothers gave her entry into Friar Park where she took a number of pictures inside. That was interesting.

I decided to forego Sunday. There's only so much that even a staunch Beatles fan can take and two days was just about enough for me.

As far as I know, there has not been a Beatles fan convention in Minnesota since.

⌒

To bring it back to Mimi for a moment, she could never understand the attraction that these conventions held. She felt that the poor fans were being taken advantage of by the dealers and those who charged exorbitant prices for entry (Barb's was not one of them). To her it was a case of The Beatles having been popular and it was fine to buy their records and to have gone to their concerts but after that it was simply a case of others making money off of them and she never approved of that no matter who it was. She didn't grasp the whole fan phenomena.....yet.

In fact, until John died, I don't think Mimi completely grasped just how gigantic their popularity really was. She heard the horror stories from John, read the newspapers and magazines, and saw it on television. But she never truly experienced it or understood it.

Eighteen

1980 started off with Paul McCartney finding himself in a Japanese jail for nine days. I could almost hear Mimi "*tsk-ing*" thousands of miles away. "*What Paul must realize is that he is not above the law. I only hope he will be man enough and accept he has been caught and not make ridiculous excuses, as previously, that he didn't know it was 'pot' or that someone 'planted' it on him.*" That was from her first letter of the new decade.

Mimi also talked about "Birth of The Beatles", the Dick Clark television movie that had recently been shown in America. She knew nothing about it and next to nothing about Pete Best, who had helped with the movie. She had only met Pete Best once, fleetingly, but wondered how any-one could know more than she about the beginning of The Beatles. "*….it was at my house it started. They met there and did a bit of practice. If anyone knows more about their beginning, I'd like to meet them.*"

She bemoaned the fact that people, who knew nothing, were making money off their false knowledge and thought it was time for all of it to stop; that The Beatles themselves should be content to take a "back seat" and let the legend go on and speak for them.

⟜⟶

*M*imi had talked to John (before the Paul news had broken) and determined that he would never tour again. He and Paul had just spoken on the phone and Paul had been complaining "*how hard the tour was*". So John had asked him "*why the hell do you do it then?*" The honest answer, according to Mimi, was that he simply could not give up the publicity.

She spoke briefly of another nephew, David, who had been down to visit just the day before. He had taken a break from his job in Saudi Arabia and would be going back for another 12 months. Like any good aunt, she worried about the unrest in that area of the world and wished he wasn't going back.

Marie had recently sent her an enlarged picture of Mimi and nephew Michael, who had been there the last time Marie had visited, and Mimi sent it on to John. He had been pleased, which she found amusing considering his continuous complaints about her "*favorites*".

⟜⟶

*M*imi was well-versed in any number of subjects, one of which was American politics. Around this time she couldn't help but bring up Ronald Reagan. "…
We are about bored to death with your election. Of the two, I hope Carter

gets in. The sight of Reagan with his dyed hair and dangerous wooley outbursts, makes you fear for what could happen. For what happens in the U.S. effects us, either directly or indirectly. It seems strange that such a wonderful country cannot find a real leader. Mind you, we are no better! Fact is, they are all played out. A real leader will emerge in both countries. They had better emerge pretty quick, but he will, in time. Meanwhile we have to meander on. Last night's confrontation (debate) was called 'The Biggest Flop'. I refuse to look or listen to any more, either U.S. or here."

And there was always time to criticize those wretched dealers. *"Marie sent me a copy of.....an article on buying and selling Beatle things. Well, I don't know......but I do know I've thrown out better things than these silly people are paying dollars for. It's a racket. These stall holders are the beneficiaries....there seems to be money in it. Now why didn't someone descend on me with copious dollars before I threw such a lot out. No, there's something distasteful about the whole bang lot. I don't believe half the things are genuine."*

Double Fantasy had been made and was also a topic of conversation. *"I do hope the record is good. He said it was good. Well, says I, you've made some stinkers. 'Yes' says he."*

⌒

John sent her a silver box from Tiffany's in honor of the album. Inscribed on top was "Double Fantasy 1980". It was post marked December 8th.

Nineteen

The weekend before was a typical winter weekend in Minnesota. Friends called and asked if I'd like to accompany them to northern Minnesota to look at cabins. Huh? Well, actually, they said they were going to get a pair of skis for the kids. It was a marketing scheme. Come look at one of the cabins and you'll get a free pair of skis. I made a deal with them. If the male in the family would pick me up a copy of Playboy with the John interview, I would go.

My power was something back in those days. And it worked. Five adults and two kids piled into the sedan that Saturday. The magazine was passed around to everyone to read. I got it last.

It was an odd weekend. I'd had a feeling of real foreboding for several days before and it seemed only to grow. I mentioned it to my friends and they tried to convince me it was just my job and the upcoming holidays. I rather doubted it, but there didn't seem any other logical explanation so I let it go.

That Monday, the 8th, it was snowing but I decided to go out during my lunch hour to mail my cards and get the final bit of Christmas shopping done. But mostly I wanted to run to Dayton's Department Store and pick up Double Fantasy.

When I got home that night the first thing I did was sit down on the floor and take the album out of its sleeve. Putting it gently on the turn table I sat back to listen. The ding ding ding of the Tibetan bells on the first song was familiar. They'd been playing (Just Like) Starting Over for several weeks already on the radio. But the other songs on the album were all new and I was somewhat disappointed that Yoko had half the songs. I hadn't acquired a taste for her music. I still haven't for that matter.

I talked to several friends that night on the phone and talked about the album almost exclusively. "*I like half of it a lot*" was my initial critique.

By 10:30 I was getting ready for bed when the phone rang. It wasn't entirely strange for it to ring that late, just a little. I picked it up to hear:

Kathy?" It was my friend Mary who I'd already spoken to that evening.

"*Yeah?*"

"*John's dead.*"

"*John?.....John who?*"

"*Lennon! They just interrupted the football game to announce it.*"

My first thought, with apologies now to John, was that he had overdosed. "*How?*"

"*He was shot.*"

"*Shot?!*" Then I thought of a robbery. Maybe someone had broken into the Dakota.

"*Outside the Dakota. That's all I've heard. Turn on the TV.*"

I hung up the phone and sat down on the bed for a moment. John Lennon was dead. John Lennon was dead? No, that couldn't be right. And if it was right, shouldn't there be something I should be doing? Perhaps it's the Scandinavian Minnesotan inside me, but my first thought was that I should bring a hot dish to Mimi. Seriously.

I went to turn on the television but before I could get that far the phone starting ringing, and continued ringing all night long. I think I had my last phone call at 5:00 the following morning. I heard from everyone I would have expected to hear from, but then there were others like a boy I had been in high school with. He was a photographer and had been a friend of Tony Glover (one third of Turner, Ray & Glover, friend of Bob Dylan, and all night DJ on KDWB). He had borrowed all my Beatles Monthlies for some kind of Beatle special that was being done in the early 70's and had never returned them. He promised that night that he would. He still hasn't. And there was an old friend from Duluth that I hadn't heard from in years. She found me that night, too, though I've since lost her again.

By 6 a.m. I put down the phone and got up to get ready for work. I didn't want to go, but I was out of cigarettes (I was a smoker back then, and very much so that night) and had to go out to buy more anyway. Actually I think back now and realize I was just functioning out of habit that morning.

I made a cup of coffee and finally got around to turning on the television. I had turned it on the night before between phone calls and can remember seeing a babbling Geraldo Rivera being interviewed for some reason and then switching it off again. But I can remember that morning distinctly. It was CBS, and whatever their morning show was called at the time. They were playing a film clip of John sitting at the white piano singing Imagine. That's when it hit me. John Lennon was dead. I sank to my knees in tears.

⌒

*L*ater that day Barb, of The Write Thing, called me at work and asked if I could come over. The press was at her house and she needed some help. They also wanted to talk to a John fan. I wasn't sure I wanted to talk to the press, but I left during my lunch hour anyway (never to return that day, though the people I worked with didn't know that).

I remember it was snowing that day – hard – but I barely noticed it as I drove to St. Paul. I had the radio on and no matter what button I pushed they were either talking about John or playing his music. It was heartbreaking.

I also remember there was a reporter from the Minneapolis Star Tribune at Barb's when I arrived. Barb must have told him I knew Mimi because he asked me if I had talked to her yet. No. I hadn't. But I had talked to my friend Judy and she had called her. Mimi had told her that Michael was coming for her and he was taking her back to Liverpool. I assumed she was there by now and I didn't know how to reach her up there. Then he asked me something somewhat peculiar, I thought. Did I think John was really dead or might it be some kind of ruse, similar to what the rumors about Jim Morrison's death had been?

"*No. He's dead.*" John would never have faked that kind of death simply to "get away". He'd already been away for five years. He wasn't on the island with Marilyn and JFK. What had happened last night in New York City, was just as real as what had happened in Dallas.

The reporter finally left but I didn't go back to work. I just didn't want to. Instead I sat with Barb for a while, during which time Louise Harrison phoned and wanted to make sure Barb put a message in her next newsletter about the grief she was feeling for John and how her sympathies went out to John's family and fans. Or something like that. Barb had written the statement down and we had immediately lost it and not on purpose. I swear!

Later that night everyone gathered at my apartment to watch the news and the televised tributes that were on. That was the night we saw our first glimpse of Paul on the news where he muttered the infamous *"it's a drag"* comment. I viewed it differently from a lot of people apparently. I immediately thought he appeared to be in shock and looked totally devastated. I, for one, had never seen him look quite like that before.

A local television station tracked Barb down at my apartment and asked if they could come over to interview her. As they lugged their equipment down the hall, I went into my bedroom and closed the door in order to return a few phone calls.

When I finally emerged an hour later, the news crew had left and I was informed that they had waited for quite a while for me to come out. Barb had told them I knew Mimi and they wanted to talk to me about her. Oh well.

I was at work the following day (Wednesday) when I received a phone call from Marie. She had phoned

John's cousin, Michael, that morning and was given the phone number of his mother Anne's house where Mimi was staying. She had phoned and talked to Mimi and was calling me now to tell me that Mimi wanted to talk to me. She gave me the phone number and I said I would run home at noon and phone her, but deep down I was not looking forward to it at all. It was enough to know that she was okay. What could I possibly say to her? There was nothing that would even begin to ease the pain I knew she was feeling.

When I finally phoned, it was Mimi herself that answered the phone.

She sounded drained but she didn't cry. I was glad of that because then I would have cried and we'd get nowhere. I told her how sorry I was and she wanted to know if I knew anything because they'd heard nothing there (I assumed she meant from New York). I told her about the ten minutes of silence that had been announced and she wanted to know what that meant. I explained what I took it to mean but she seemed confused by it all. Looking back now I think she was wondering about a funeral or a memorial service. She said later that she never would have been able to go to New York but if there had been an actual service, I wonder.

That night I attended a candlelight vigil at the University of Minnesota with friends. There were only a couple hundred people there but it was also painfully cold and the event was held outside. The vigil had a rather calming effect. I was surrounded by people feeling just as bad as I was. We weren't alone in our grief. It made a difference.

I remember seeing on the news sometime that week over 30,000 people at a vigil in Canada. 30,000 people strong! It seemed that not only was his death unbelievable, but so was the reaction. Day after day it headlined the evening news; that, too, unheard of.

When the candlelight vigil ended we went somewhere to get a bite to eat. There was a paper left in the booth, filled with John. It was the first time in several years that I saw a picture of Julian. He was leaving his home in Wales to go to NY. Everybody knows the picture. His resemblance to John could not have been more startling at that moment.

⌒

I talked to Mimi briefly again on Friday mainly to see how she was. She was more tearful then and I believe it was during that conversation that she said she knew nothing of what was going on in New York, but it was *"no matter. John is gone and none of that matters anymore."*

I kept in touch the entire time she was in Liverpool. I remember telling her how remarkable the reaction was here and that there were dozens of magazines coming out every week that were either dedicated to John or contained lengthy articles about him. If she'd like them, I would be willing to send some over. She said she would like to see them so I made a trip to the post office with rather a heavy bundle of magazines several days later.

⌒

*C*hristmas came and went that year. I hardly remember it. But I did attend a small get-together at Barb's house on New Year's Eve Day. It was then she told us she had received a phone call from someone representing MDC who wanted to know the value of the autographed Double Fantasy album that John had signed for the maniac.

Already it was starting.

Twenty

imi was home by January and her first letter to me was dated 19th of January:

Dear Kathy,

Forgive me not writing. I thank you for your kind thoughts.

I'm completely devastated and find it so hard to accept. The night before he was on the phone for an hour. It was the same "old John". Funny and happy, telling me he was coming and couldn't wait to see me.

I've just had a phone call from Judy. She's going to phone you to-night. I've had so many letters and cards from girls. I don't know them and no addresses so if you know of any would you thank them for me. Marie phoned to Anne's house. Michael gave her the number. All so kind. I could never thank any of you enough. It meant a lot.

Michael tells me there's a lot of rubbish written about him but I won't read any of it. Mostly if not all untrue. It was amazing how the American magazines knew where I was. Phone, phone, phone but for-tunately Michael arrived at 10:30 a.m. and got rid of all the press with their cameras and we set off for Anne's house right away. Nobody knew where I was so I was glad of that.

There is to be a service in Liverpool Cathedral on 29ᵗʰ March. All tickets have gone. I won't be going. I might and probably would start crying. I couldn't bear anyone to see me.

Tell Marie I'll write to her.

God Bless.

Love, Mimi x

If she was following the five stages of grief, by March she was experiencing anger.

"*...Your welcome letter this morning...and Ringo's article. At least he felt enough to attempt to visit the Dakota. The others – nothing, either to me or anyone else. I did think, when I could think a bit, -- not a word from Paul. I expect he knew I knew too much about his attempts to discredit John re the songs and music. The attempt failed. How could it succeed? John was pleased about that when he phoned me about it. In his usual way, bore no malice toward Paul. It was settled and that was that. I don't think I really expected to hear from the others but I did hear from Ringo's mother, a warm comforting kind woman whose one thought was for me, but she was always thoughtful for me. I didn't bother with the others families. The whole thing went to their head, but not Ringo's mother.......*

"*.......After years of battling to be noticed and fighting desperately to be first, now the opportunity has arrived! The centre of notice and attention. At what a cost! Seemingly reveling in it, not a sign of emotion as far as I could detect in conversation on the phone. It will go on. Doesn't she realize the real centre of attention has gone? She knows she was tolerated because of him. God knows nobody would have heard of* *her…..Meanwhile, all I know is he's gone and at time I think I'll go mental. Some days I am more or less able to go on, then I'm devastated and lost……..*

"…….Another thing, Kathy, I'm not at all impressed by Julian. Why has he gone to live with her? She said she was getting him tutored on drums. He could get that here. Sending him out to buy clothes, etc. That's all I got on the phone, and bringing his girlfriend over. More of what a "wonderful kind person I am". He may make a drummer, but brain – NO. It's the easy way out. Poor misguided John. So naïve and so talented, never could see through people. He didn't come home all these years because she was not accepted. When I last spoke to him he was so full of life and "coming home", although he would always love America and the people and live there, but naturally part of him was always here. It was better for Sean in America, to grow up in a mixed racial society. It's much harder here. I haven't heard from her since – too busy enjoying and attracting attention…..

"…..To my great surprise I had a letter from Paul's stepmother. I had only seen her once briefly. Whatever happened between her and Paul and the McCartneys, she sounded very bitter and has a bad time financially – broke, in fact. It sounds bad but she didn't go into it in detail but I'm not too surprised really. She was very kind tho about me and John.

One thing – I wasn't wanted in America at this dreadful time. I might have attracted some attention. I couldn't have gone, Kathy, it would have been the end of me, but I wasn't given the chance – very cool, calm and collected when I felt I would go completely mad. All the money in the world will not make her a pop star or more acceptable, only to those who have an eye on the main chance and hope to gain. There will be plenty of that type hanging on…

"…Julian's place is with his mother – not looking for a soft spot. Please god, she will not influence him with her peculiar ideas. He will have all the money with no effort on his part it seems to me. That's all

he wants. Not good for anyone who has shown no "shape" in any way. But – what the hell! What do I care when it comes down to it…..

"……It's so hard to accept and believe……..

"….Marie sent me a copy of Philip Norman's book. It, as usual, was very kind of her. Philip Norman sent me a copy "with the author's compliments". I went through it and in a short time I was jumping mad. I've sent it back to him with acid comments written on nearly every page……It's all rewrites from the "yellow press". How dare he say John was brought up in a 'tough working class district". My husband serving milk! George was the 3rd generation of farmers. They had 10 cowmen, milking Machines, etc. My father a "white collar dandy" "L'pool Pilot!" He was a wise old sea dog and would scorn to be called a "white collar dandy". Pity John couldn't answer him! He was absolutely fed up with being called 'rough working class' and said so in his last interview. Kathy, there's nothing wrong with being working class, everyone who works is working class, but when I think of the careful upbringing John had, the best of education, wanting for nothing. In fact the others envied him – everything at first. That he wasted most of his school time, I admit, but he was talented and was bound to do something, school or no school. It was there, bound to come out one way or another. As far those school friends – Peter Shotten and Ivan Vaughn, they were born cadgers and hangers on. He had to get rid of them eventually. Now they too have done their best to say anything bad. If he was so bad, where was I with my hawk eye that never saw drink, bad behavior to such an extent. Liela came down to see me and I showed her the book. Drunk I never saw, he is not and never has been a drinker, but she is furious. Several patients at the surgery after consultation said to her "wasn't John terrible!" She was giving a lecture at the University on cancer, and several doctors also said similar things. "What a shock for Mimi to get to know all these things about John." It was humiliating for her as she is a very clever doctor and has an important position in the medical profession and was very

close to John. He used to visit her when she was studying at Edinburgh University. I was sorry for her and like a raving lunatic myself…."

Letters like that would arrive every few weeks. She resented the press so much and the books that were being published she considered treasonous. The latest was 'Shout' by Philip Norman. And, of course, the subject of Paul McCartney never having gotten in touch with her was always in the back of her mind.

"…..I was talking to Neil Aspinall – Apple. He too is furious about the book 'Shout', such a pathetic liar for money. I had a good 'shout' about Paul, too. Behold! A couple of hours later a phone call from Paul! He was nervous of me…I told you…..many excuses. Thought I was annoyed with him. And so I was. Also Paul seriously thinking of going after Philip Norman over 'Shout'. If ever I see Philip Norman I'll pitch into him. Paul advised me not to do it myself. It is monstrous that this scandal monger can write such things."

I was delighted that Paul had phoned but there was another part to her letter that surprised me even more.

"I was rather alarmed when Judy told me she was coming over in September – alone. I think it unwise to come alone, you know, it can be very lonely in another country alone, with no one you know or can really talk to. I don't know what her plans are. She won't be coming just to see me. All the same, I feel quite worried.

"Now – this part I hesitate lest I offend you ---- Kathy, would you accept help towards you coming with her? It would be such a lovely opportunity to see you together. It would give me great pleasure and I can easily send help, no bother at all. All you have to do is let me know. Judy said it was expensive. I didn't like to ask her how much, it was not a

long phone call. I immediately tried to phone you, but no reply. It was dead. I had a number for you, 612 533 but I must have missed some numbers. I tried several times. Do discuss it with Judy and do consider it…..Please don't be offended. It's purely selfish on my part. Just a 'little help from and between friends'…..Now just think, just the 3 of us, you and me smoking…..and talking. I'll drop dead if I have offended you. I look forward to hearing good news from you."

Offend me? Not even close! I had to read over that part of the letter at least a dozen times. She wanted to help pay my way over to England! Get away! I had no intention of allowing her to do so, but the offer was exciting.

I phoned Judy that night. Not too surprising, she said she wanted to travel to England alone this time. She'd always traveled with someone else and this time she wanted to do it alone. I understood. And there was already a Plan B. I had a friend who was from England and whose sister was getting married in August. She'd asked me to come with her to the wedding and I'd not yet given her an answer.

By later that night, I had told Lindsay I would go with her, had called Mimi to tell her I was coming in August, and invited another friend, Mary, along for the ride. Mary had in-laws living there that she wanted to see. I would spend our first week in England with Mimi. Then we would all meet in Birmingham the second week for the wedding.

I was going back to England!

Twenty One

etters flew back and forth that summer. We were somewhat making plans for my visit, but a lot of it was just Mimi being Mimi and between the suggestions to travel light and a warning that she won't be the same; that the events of the previous December had taken their toll, she would come up with surprising news. First there had been the phone call from Paul. A letter dated 19th June, 1981 brought up another surprise call.

"7p.m. last night the phone went, I was half expecting an American voice, but no – It was definitely a L'pool voice. Slightly, but L'pool anyway. I knew it was not my family, we all have the similar voice. I kept saying who? Who? Who are you? Then I nearly dropped dead (kidding). The voice said 'It's Cyn'. I could hardly believe it. She started to tell me about Twist, marriage finished, he's had 3 affairs, one after another. Apart from that I don't know what the call was for. So taken aback that ME, Mimi, didn't say anything. She would come down, see me, etc. etc. and – I'm not much wiser. Since then I've been so puzzled,

wondering why she phoned me. I didn't even get her phone no., or address, and no idea how to get it unless I try enquiries. She may not be under Twist......I wouldn't put it past her to use Lennon. Think I'll try. I want to ask her why she phoned, any reason especially. Can there be any motive? She's determined to keep in the news one way or another. It's puzzling, but I would not be any use to her.

"I know Cyn says she wants to hide away. God knows why. All the time she gets in touch with the press....I know she does not like [fans] and until I picked all the fan letters out of the dust bin and answered them, every fan letter was destroyed. So I answered which infuriated her, but I didn't care. The girls got an answer. John knew nothing about it.

"I'll keep this open and try to get Cyn's number, and find out. The more I think of it, the more puzzled I am. There's some reason I feel sure.

"I told my sister about [a fan] saying Mrs. Powell was a 'gem', and she said 'What! That awful woman a gem! And her sly daughter – have nothing to do with that lot, well rid of them.' We'll have a talk when you come. If I wrote....and wrote all, there would be a different complexion on the image, I can tell you!

(Next day) "Just talking to Anne. She said 'don't bother finding where Cyn is. There's some motive why she phoned after all these years. She could have phoned in Dec. And why these undying declarations of great love for John.' If that was so, why chase the Italian, who by the way is totally ignored. She's had 2 husbands since John. Anne feels there is money in it. Some funny business going on. I'm not interested in any money. It's bad enough he's gone.

"It's not a good example to Julian to encourage him to go into pubs. He does not impress me at all. Seems lazy and aimless trying to cash in on his father's image. John said he had no brain. Sounds as though he was right. Cyn should direct him to doing something instead of hanging

around doing absolutely nothing. She trying to be the same age in outlook. It can't be done. She's to blame for him being aimless, but there's no time for children when you're looking for new husbands, and looking for a good time."

Twenty Two

I wasn't nearly as nervous going to England this time. It was my second time, after all. I was practically a pro! And one of my travel mates was English. I could just follow Lindsay around like a little puppy and she would always know what to do. Except she was going to Birmingham straight away and I was going to Bournemouth in the opposite direction.

Mary's relatives met her at Gatwick and I hitched a ride with them to Southampton. At least we were headed in the right direction. Mary had said if I flirted enough I might get her cousin-in-law to take me all the way to Bournemouth. Apparently I should have worn a shorter skirt because I got as far as the train station in Southampton and that was it.

Before that though, I can remember on the ride we curved around the roads of a beautiful English countryside and suddenly there was a castle. It was slightly decayed and sitting all by itself in a huge field, but it was a castle. You can drive all day in Minnesota and look at a multitude of lakes and the blessed wild life but you will never see a castle. Not one.

It was on the train to Bournemouth, sitting all alone and keeping an eye on my luggage that I pondered at what an adult thing I was doing; traveling through England. Just me and my suitcase.

It was approximately 1:00 in the afternoon when I arrived in Poole and I had a vague realization that I had been up for close to 24 hours now. Mimi hurried out the front door to pay for the taxi and making sure that cabbie knew he was charging too much in the process.

Next was our actual greeting on the terrace. It was so good to see her again and after her hug, I once again knew there was nothing to be nervous about. She was the same Mimi; a few years older and Lord knew she'd had the stuffing kicked out of her just a few months before, but basically still warm and welcoming.

She had me put my suitcase in "John's room" and I changed into something a little more comfortable after traveling all day. When I emerged she was busy in the kitchen, informing me that Sunday dinner would be ready momentarily.

We talked informally at first; how was your flight, where were the other girls now, had I taken the train all the way to Poole from London? That's when I told her I had caught the train in Southampton and had gotten off in Bournemouth. She laughed. She had scolded the cab driver because she thought he'd taken me from the Poole station which was only a few minutes away. She felt for sure that I knew to get off in Poole. And here I thought I had been so adult and done everything right. Ah well.

Once we had finished dinner and I helped with clearing the table, we both sat down and had our after-dinner cigarettes and tea. That's when the subject turned to John. I know I hadn't come out and asked her anything in particular because I hadn't been sure how I'd bring the subject up, but she began by talking about all the mail she had received after he had been killed. That was the beginning of an almost week-long homily on John Lennon.

She had received hundreds of letters from all over the world. One, she said, had been from Barbara Walters and another from Senator Edward Kennedy. She had never spoken particularly well of Ted Kennedy in the past, though she adored JFK. Her opinion of the younger Kennedy was heavily influenced by his association with the Irish IRA. But as she spoke about him now I could tell her feelings for him had done an about-turn. His letter had been very kind.

Mimi said she had received a packet of photographs of John from Linda McCartney. They were from the White Album photo shoot. Mimi didn't care for any of those particular photos. She thought John look horrible in each and every one. It didn't take away from the kindness of sending them, she said, but they weren't photos she'd be keeping. She also found it somewhat odd that the pictures came on their own with no letter or note.

Many of the fans who had written had included pictures of John but she was finding them too hard to look at. She had even taken down the large portrait that Astrid had taken that hung in the sitting room above the stereo. The stereo itself had been moved to a different room.

s we took our tea into the sitting room, I asked her how she'd heard the horrible news. All the reports seemed to indicate that Yoko had phoned Mimi, Paul and Julian. Mimi said it had been much later when she'd heard from Yoko. Instead she awoke early that morning and had the BBC World News on her radio. When she heard the name John Lennon mentioned, she wondered what he had done now. She had no time to comprehend the words that followed before the telephone rang.

It was Neil Aspinall, she said. He'd barely gotten the word "*Mimi?*" out when he burst into tears.

"*NO!*" she had screamed back at him in anger and threw the phone back into its cradle.

As the press began to show up, knocking at the door, she found herself staring blankly into a mirror and cutting great hunks of her hair off, completely unaware of what she was doing or why. Her nephew Michael called and said he was coming for her so she spent the rest of the morning getting ready to go to Liverpool. Through it all, she felt as if she were walking through a bizarre nightmare and nothing about that day seemed real.

'd been awake about 36 hours by the time I fell into "John's bed" that night. My friend Mary had given me a blank book to use as a diary on the trip, but I was simply too exhausted to write. I fell asleep that night cursing the fact that there's no way I would remember everything and wishing I had a tape recorder instead of the damn book! If life were fair, it should include a video recorder.

⌒

*M*imi was already up when I finally rolled out of that comfortable bed the next morning. She had a lovely breakfast waiting and as I sat down to enjoy it, we took up where we'd left off the night before; talking about John.

We talked about John almost entirely that week. It had taken his death for her to take a larger interest in the Beatle side of him. This was eight months after his death and she insinuated that there were very few people to talk about him to. Her family had moved on it seemed, and she was left alone miles and miles away from them anyway. This was her choice though. She preferred living where she did; somewhat elusive with only a few friends in the area. There was always the telephone if she wanted to talk.

She spoke about John's mother one night without any real prompting. She had been talking about reporters and how one had been so rude as to ask her if John wasn't her real son, why she'd never adopted John as her own. Her response to him had been *"I'm sure you don't mean to be so impertinent"* but to me she gave an explanation.

The subject of adoption had apparently come up in the early years and Mimi would have liked nothing more. Julia's permission would not have been a problem, she said, but she absolutely refused to make any effort to track down Alfred Lennon and had no desire to ever talk to him again. For all intent and purposes John was hers anyway so she never gave it a great deal thought after that.

She spoke warmly of Julia despite what movies and books have portrayed. Julia was her favorite sister, Mimi said.

Later she wrote *"Julia married this Lennon on 3rd December, 1938. Nobody knew anything about them. John was born on 9th October 1940. No one in the family were at the wedding, knew nothing about it until Julia came in with a wedding certificate and that was that. This Lennon was not allowed in or near the house. My Father forbade her to have anything to do with him. She just thought it was clever to defy the family at the time. She soon regretted it when she realized it was not so clever.*

"Julia was a beautiful girl, headstrong. The only good thing out of it was John and I took him almost immediately. I loved Julia. She was so witty and amusing, always laughing. We all make mistakes. Julia's was not realizing the seriousness of a defiant 'prank'. We were all shocked. It was not as though she had to be married. Nothing of the kind. Just defiance against the family refusing to accept him. A most unsuitable person in every way."

After Julia was killed, Mimi said she was never able to go to her gravesite. It was simply too painful. Julia's grave and her own mother's; she never visited either one.

Yet when Mimi first heard the song 'Julia' she was deeply hurt. She had no idea he was going to write a song like that and was floored when she heard it. Her sisters told her it was her own fault for never having told John the truth and always doting on him too much, and that she should sit down and tell him the truth then and there. I was never told in exact words what that "truth" was but she said she finally told him everything during the last year of his life and that he eventually thanked her profusely for all she'd done for him. Mimi figured that it was due to Sean and everything John was now having to do that gave him an understanding of what she had gone through.

I never did find out what that "truth" was about Julia. It was almost as if she assumed I already knew. But I didn't and I never asked.

⟵⟶

*S*he also told me an interesting story about The Beatles break-up that I'd never heard before and have yet to see verified anywhere or by anyone. But I'll tell it anyway.

It seems that while negotiating different things during the breaking up, John worried most about George. He figured Ringo could always make a living being Ringo, but he wasn't sure about George. So he suggested to Paul that they each give him a percentage of the Lennon/McCartney songs. George and Ringo were already receiving an equal share but this would be a little extra just for George.

Paul refused, and was totally adamant about it. They argued about it for days. So finally John threw his hands up in defeat and made arrangements for George to receive a percentage directly out of John's pocket, leaving Paul out of it.

The reason John was so angry at George at the end of his life had nothing to do with not being mentioned in George's autobiography but because George had never thanked him. John had given him the money, there had almost been a huge row with Paul over it, and he had never been thanked.

I'm just the messenger, folks.

Twenty Three

We took the bus into Bournemouth one morning. Despite my telling her just the opposite, she was far too concerned about my visit not being interesting enough and wanted to show me the city. Showing me the city mainly consisted of going through one of the larger department stores where she immediately told me to pick out something that she could buy me by which to remember my visit.

The store was large and busy that day and there really was nothing I needed or felt comfortable asking for. Just a few weeks before, though, Charles and Diana had been married and all the various souvenirs were still on display.

She moved right past the vulgar plates and trivets to a table of silk scarves. She sorted through them until she found a lovely blue with the Prince of Wales insignia in the center and the names of Charles and Diana and the date of their marriage bordering all four sides. It really was quite beautiful.

"Here. Do you like this one?" she asked.

I did indeed but also noticed it was £15.

"That's too much, Mimi."

"If you like it, then I'll get it. Don't worry about the cost."

And I still have that silk scarf.

From there it was on to a small lunch and then back home again.

⟨⟩

I t was that afternoon that she talked about Paul and the time he had phoned her back in April. Mimi had truly been upset that he'd not called her before then and she had bent Neil Aspinall's ear one Sunday afternoon. Two hours later all was forgiven with a phone call from Paul. She said she scolded him, telling him he should have known she wasn't thinking of any ridiculous slight he might have been worried about. It had been John who had been killed and Paul should have known she was thinking of nothing else. I don't know what he said but they both cried, she said, and any resentment was gone.

She said she could hear children in the background and asked him if all those were his. *"Yeah, we're like rabbits around here."*

They discussed the book *Shout!* by Philip Norman and how they resented parts of it. He told her not to get involved and that he would handle it, though what he intended on doing or what he actually did, I have no idea. Since Norman is now writing a biography on Paul and claims to have received a rather conceptual OK, I would assume all is forgiven there as well.

Before ringing off, Paul said he would be down to visit her one day; something she was still waiting to see happen.

The Guitar's All Right as a Hobby, John

~~~

There were no photographs of John or anyone else around the house except for a small one of me in a frame on her desk. I assumed it had been positioned there just before I arrived. She wasn't able to look at any pictures of John, she explained. It was still too painful. The topic of photographs got us onto the subject of Sean.

John had made it abundantly clear after Sean was born that he didn't want photo sessions set up with his son in them, and that the fewer pictures taken the better. I told her that apparently his decree was followed because I had seen very few pictures of Sean in the five years since he was born. Very few.

Mimi went into the other room and came back with two leather bound photo albums and a framed 8x10 of Sean. John had sent her the photographs. They were professionally taken and they were beautiful. She kept them in a drawer, though, in case any fans showed up since that had been John's wishes. This, of course, was before Sean started hanging out with and appearing in short movies with Michael Jackson.

~~~

We were having a late dinner that night. John had always said he loved her chips so that's what we ended up having. Chips and tea.

We were sitting at the table, talking about nothing in particular, when suddenly there was a knock at the door. I quickly glanced at the clock. 9:00. Who comes calling at 9:00 at night?

"Why don't you get the door, dear," Mimi suggested.

I must have looked hesitant because she smiled with a little twinkle in her eye. *"Go on. Paul said he'd visit. It might be him."*

I can't imagine what my face must have looked like. A hundred things flew through my mind. Paul? Paul McCartney might be at the door and she wanted me to answer it. Sure. No problem.

"Go on then."

I pulled myself away from the table and started for the front door. *"I'll answer it but if it's him, I'm hiding in the bathroom."* She loved that.

I opened the door but it was not Paul McCartney.

Twenty Four

His name was David and he had traveled from London to meet Mimi. Or maybe he had come down to Bournemouth on holiday and decided to include a visit with Mimi. I really don't remember. But to sweeten the deal, he brought a beautiful bouquet of flowers for her. She said to let him in and as he joined us at the table she offered him a cup of tea.

He was a Beatle fan from way back and told us tales of the various events he had witnessed; one of the more interesting being when he'd been in the crowd when John and Yoko had appeared in court after being arrested for possession of the dreaded marijuana. I later looked up a picture and, sure enough, there he was.

I don't recall if he said he was working in the music business at the time or not, but I've since seen pictures of him with Sir Paul being honored as a Companion of LIPA so he's moving on up.

That night, though, he was in awe of the photo of Sean that had inadvertently remained on the sideboard when we had been looking at photos earlier. I cringed a bit when he took pictures of the picture since it was still assumed Sean would remain out of sight until at least the ripe old age of six. But David went ahead with the pictures anyway and in the end what did it matter?

I got to watch Mimi in action, joining in the Beatle talk. At one point David had asked her if John had ever actually returned to England after settling in New York. Being rather cagey herself, she said that he had come back and never been noticed because he had often used disguises, one being that of the Artful Dodger from the play Oliver. And why had he come back? Well, to see her, of course.

Because I was sitting there, probably with a confused look on my face, she simply smiled at me. I knew John had never returned. At least not to see her. I could count the number of times he had promised to come back for a visit and never appeared. When I asked her later why she had said that, she simply shrugged. *"It doesn't matter."*

And perhaps it didn't. But when I tried to explain to David later that, despite what she said, John had never returned, he went on to argue that he had told Derek Taylor at a Liverpool convention what Mimi had said and Taylor said if Mimi had said it, then it was true.

People wonder how all the false info gets started.

T he sad thing about the whole John coming back story, was I think he honestly intended to do so in 1981. Mimi told me many times before he died that he would tell her how anxious he was to return and show Sean all the places of his youth. It was something he had even told her in their last conversation, the night before he died.

⌒

But back to The Beatles fan, David was going to visit Brownsea Island ~ also in Poole ~ the following day and invited me along. I think Mimi accepted for me, continually worrying that my visit wasn't exciting enough.

So the following day was spent seeing Brownsea Island. Thirty-two years later, I can't remember a whole lot about it except I saw one of Sir Walter Raleigh's ships in the harbor and on the ferry over to the island, I saw my first real punker; colored Mohawk, rings through the nose, the whole nine yards. I only wish I'd had the nerve to ask him if I could take his picture.

When we returned to Mimi's, it was somehow mentioned that we were having lunch with friends of hers, the Richardsons, the following day. David offered to drive us there, and so he did.

Before we leave the subject of David, though, I must mention how he got in touch with me when I returned home and it wasn't too long before a large envelope arrived in the mail one day. It was a large program from one of Linda's photography showings and it had been autographed by Paul, Linda, Michael McCartney, his soon-to-be wife Rowena, Kate Robbins, and David! A very nice surprise indeed! And yes, I still have that, too.

The Richardsons were a lovely couple that had known Mimi since she moved to Dorset. Apparently Mimi had been a little loose with her description of me as the first thing Mrs. Richardson said was *"this is little Kathy?"* I stood nearly 5'9" and was the tallest one in the room.

"You said a little Beatle fan was coming to visit."

"Oh I think of all of the girls as little. It's hard for me to realize they've all grown up."

We had a lovely lunch where I was peppered with questions about Minnesota. Where was it located (*"right in the middle of the States on the Canadian border"*). Is there anything famous there that they would have heard about. (*"Oh gosh, let's see. Hubert Humphrey, the Vice President under Lyndon Johnson was from there. Judy Garland…..Bob Dylan…."*). The mere mention of Dylan brought a disgusted look from Mimi.

As we finished up lunch and went into the sitting room, the subject of Mimi's china came up. She had told me earlier that week that she had sent all her china to John because he had asked for it, and now that he was gone, she wanted it back. I had seen it the first time I'd visited in 1973 and it was a beautiful Royal Albert, lovely pink and yellow flowers in the design. Mrs. Richardson asked her why she simply didn't call Yoko and ask for it. When Mimi waved that suggestion off, Mrs. Richardson then offered to call Yoko for her. No, she would handle it, Mimi insisted, but I have to wonder if she ever got it back. I rather doubt it. When I left her after that visit, she gave me the one piece she had kept back, a small relish dish.

Like old friends do, they began reminiscing and Mrs. Richardson started a story about when John and Cynthia had come down to visit back in the 60's. They had either been taken to the Richardsons or the Richardsons were at Mimi's, but the subject of the Richardson's son came up and the fact that he had a boat. Arrangements were made for the son to take John and Cyn out in the boat and John was beside himself with excitement.

He made Mimi make sandwiches for them so they could have a picnic somewhere along the way, and was so excited that he stood over her the entire time making sure she did everything right.

Once out in the boat, they traveled around until they found a small island. And it's there that they had their picnic. There were very few people around and John was able to enjoy himself without being bothered. When they returned, he told Mimi it was the most fun he'd ever had.

Did you know Cynthia?" Mrs. Richardson asked me.

"*No.*" I don't know anybody, I wanted to add.

"*Very sweet girl. But very quiet.*"

I'm not sure why she mentioned Cyn, but I agreed with her that that's what I'd always heard while also thinking with amusement how many people, particularly the elders, think because I knew Mimi that I would know everyone she knew. If I knew Mimi, I must know John. That type of mentality. If only.....

We stayed for an hour or so after lunch and then it was back to the bungalow on the harbor's edge.

I t was a delightfully warm day, so we went out on the terrace to sit and sip a gin and tonic. As one subject phased into another, I got the nerve to ask Mimi a question that had bothered me since December. Did she own the house? Was it in her name?

She shook her head. *"No. Everything was in John's name. All of it."*

"There's no worry about you having to move at some point, is there?"

"No. He bought it for me to live in and for the family to use for holidays."

I don't think she quite understood my meaning but I let that question drop for the moment and instead talked about the value of the house. I had been in Redondo Beach, California a couple years prior, and had condominiums pointed out that were just off the beach and were allegedly worth $3 million. Condos! When I told Mimi that she seemed skeptical.

"Really?"

"Really. I can't even begin to tell you how much your house would be worth if it were in California as close to the beach as your house is now."

"After John died, men came down and appraised all this for the estate. I doubt it came to $3 million."

"It might have, though. If you were in the States it certainly would have." I figured I'd keep going as long as she seem interested in the subject. *"You really don't have any idea of what you have here, Mimi. Not just the house but all the awards too."*

"Those old things?"

"Yeah, the awards. And the gold records. Anything of John's. It has to be in the millions. Gold records are going for thousands at auction and look how many gold records you have. And they're John Lennon's gold records."

She seemed to only have a vague concept of how much everything was worth and I don't know if that ever changed. She did put a priceless value on John's letters, however. And yet kept them in a rubber band in her desk. She did pull out one that had Polaroids of his cats. I was allowed to look the letter over and he seemed quite concerned about the cats and what they were being fed. I often wondered what happened to those cats and if Yoko had kept them.

I t wasn't long before a tourist boat came by. I read all the stories about tourist boats going by and Mimi's house being pointed out while she ran out on the terrace to shake her fist at them. Well, this time there was no fist shaking, but the boat did come by and slowed down as it drifted by the front of the house.

"Is that the boat?" I asked, knowing she'd know which boat I meant.

She glared at it. *"Terrible nuisance! Look at them staring."*

"They're probably wondering who that nobody is with John Lennon's aunt."

She liked that, but also motioned that it was time to go back in.

W e got into one of our first disagreements that night. Talking about John and his divorce from Cynthia, she mentioned that Cyn hadn't deserved the money he'd been forced to give her as a settlement. I believe the figure we were discussing was £150,000 and she thought that was far too much. I tried to explain that considering she'd been there from the beginning and through the lion's share of Beatlemania, she deserved a far greater portion of his income than that. Nope. Cyn had cheated on John first, Mimi reasoned, so it wasn't as if she'd won the pools. That was a familiar argument and I realized she was using John's argument, almost word for word.

⟨⟩

*T*hat's the night she told me how John had come down to see her, and *"sitting right in that chair"* had told her that he had found out that Cynthia had been cheating on him with *"the Italian"* and he had literally cried when he said he was getting a divorce. To this day, I have no idea who cheated on whom first, but I eventually held my tongue and the £150,000 settlement dispute was eventually forgotten; at least for the time being.

Twenty Five

hen we switched to the subject of Yoko Ono. At that point in time she claimed she never heard from Yoko and had only brief conversations with her at the time of John's murder. Before that, she had spoken to her only once when she had called her to come to London. Yoko had only been to the house the one time with John.

She reminisced about the many times she had talked to John on the phone over the last year of his life and how he told her time and time again he was coming back to see her and to show Sean where his father was from. He was coming in 1981, he'd said. I often wondered if this wasn't the same old story, where he'd pine about how much he missed England and yet never managed to come back, but Mimi seemed convinced that this time he really meant it. And that he had never returned before because Yoko would still not have been accepted. There was, she said, no mention of Yoko coming along in '81.

It was through that conversation that she began to re-call the early years of John and Yoko. *"You wouldn't believe how quickly he changed. He was as different as night and day, just like that. It was almost as if she'd put a spell on him."*

I told her that Mrs. Powell had told my friends the same thing, and was convinced he'd been the victim of some kind of evil spell. It went without saying that many of my friends and I had thought the same thing. Even his looks had changed dramatically.

"Why couldn't he have married someone like you," she pondered pensively. *"I only ever hoped he'd marry someone I could have a chat and a laugh with over a cup of tea."*

"Oh no! I couldn't have married John," I responded, truly meaning it. *"He was on a whole different plane than me."*

"Really? Well, he certainly changed from who he was. He just wasn't the same person. But he was coming around, I think," she murmured somewhat wistfully. *"He seemed ready to do things his way now."*

⌒

She talked about his trip to Bermuda a year before. He was there alone and would call her often. He had heard a bag piper playing off in the distance one night and had im-mediately grown homesick for the time he'd spent in Scotland as a youth. (Fred Seaman later gave credence to the story in his book – or perhaps, all things considered, it was Mimi giv-ing credence to Fred).

More and more she convinced herself he was coming home, but not to stay, only to visit. She knew he would never leave New York completely.

*M*imi talked about the many dreams she'd had about John since his death. In all of them they would be in one of the department stores and they'd become separated. She'd become frantic, looking all over for him, and would finally find him laying atop one of the display tables, dead.

She also spoke of looking out over the terrace at various times and seeing him laying atop the wall, staring up at the sky, with hands behind his head.

A thunderstorm was brewing that night as I went to bed, giving a somewhat eerie feeling in my bedroom. If John was ever going to show up, tonight would be the night I figured. If he did make a visit, it was after I fell asleep. Probably a good thing.

Twenty Six

*I*t was Thursday evening when my friend Mary showed up. The plan had been for the two of us to meet up at Mimi's and then take the train to Birmingham on Friday. Mary had phoned on Wednesday wondering if we couldn't meet on Friday instead because she was so tired, but I convinced her that if she came on Thursday, it would be well worth her while. I was sure she would enjoy Mimi as much as I did.

*I*t was a rather quiet day, though Mimi's doctor did arrive for an appointment and I was asked to let him in. While they talked in her bedroom, I looked at some of the books Mimi had, and was quite surprised, and delighted, to see she still had a small book on Winston Churchill that I had sent her many years before. It was just a tiny book I'd seen at a local Hallmark shop but she had thanked me profusely at the time and that's when I became aware that Mimi was an audacious reader. This trip I had given her a book about Edward VIII and Mrs. Simpson that had recently been released in the USA. I had told her about the book, which caused her to go off on the King and his paramour at great length and then regret the fact that a book like that would never be allowed in England. So I bought her a copy.

I heard in later letters that her sister Anne wished to read it as soon as Mimi had finished. I'd also given her a gold lighter with her name engraved and the date of my visit that she said her nephew David had tried to pinch. So I seemed to do all right in the gift department.

After the doctor left, I expressed my awe at a doctor actually making house calls. They had stopped that years ago in the States. And finding two bottles of milk outside the back door every morning. That was another nicety that had ended long ago over here.

She talked a little bit about health care and wondered how we did it over here (not very well). Mrs. Powell had told her how much paperwork she had filled out when she'd been to hospital while living in Canada and Mimi couldn't believe it. I told her we were probably worse than Canada by now.

Unfortunately she didn't live long enough for me to really give her an earful on the broken medical system in the States.

⌒

*I*t was that afternoon that I thought to phone the Richardsons and thank them once again for their kindness. Mimi said their number would be in her book near the phone.

The phone was located on a small table next to the stairs going upstairs, so I sat down on one of the steps and looked through the book for Richardsons. I'm not sure at which point it occurred to me to move slowly as I skimmed the book, but slow I did go. And there they were. All the numbers. Apple. John. Paul McCartney. How valuable would this book be at auction, I wondered. I knew Mimi had no concept. And as I found the number and waited for the Richardsons to answer, I glanced down at the local phonebook where Mimi had written a number and the word "Cyn" above it. Ah yes, we had a simple treasure trove of information here.

⌒

We heard Mary's taxi arrive rather late that night. She'd taken the last train from Southampton.

I quickly escorted her in and introduced her to Mimi. That's all it took. They were like old friends after that.

Mary wasn't a Beatles fan Beatles fan. But she did like them, and she knew their music, and had read a book or two at my prodding. She was, however, into art and marveled at all the various artwork Mimi had there; much of which she obtained on a trip to Italy. Not that John was ever far away in the conversation. Everything seemed to have a connection to him. It was Mary who recognized the figurine of John in the bookcase as a Lladro.

Mimi said there were very few made of each Beatle. And that must be true as I've occasionally looked since and not only could I not find any up for sale or auction, I have yet to see them even mentioned as being made.

Mimi gave Mary her bedroom which was downstairs in the front of the house. It was the room that contained all the gold records, on the walls and in the closet. Mimi took a room upstairs to sleep in.

I'd gone to bed but was still awake reading when I heard a soft knock on the door. It was Mary. As I recall, she came in somewhat overwhelmed by all the real artifacts in her room. She knew the bed I was in was John's (it must have been mentioned at some time during the evening) and asked timidly if I thought it would be all right if she sat on the edge of it.

"Oh my God! I'm sleeping in it. I doubt he'd care if you sat on it!"

She loved Mimi. She loved the fact that she was in a house belonging to John Lennon. And she was so glad she decided to come instead of spending another night in Southampton. I remember before she retired back to her room, I handed her my camera and told her to see if she could get some pictures of the gold records. Oh, and if she could get one of the Queen's Proclamation for the MBE that was in the closet, that would be cool, too.

She did.

$\smile$

$\mathcal{W}$hen I got up the next morning I found Mimi in the dining room. She had a letter in her hand and there were tears in her eyes.

"Are you all right?"

The letter was from her solicitor, she said, and it was about her will. The letter explained that she had left her entire estate to John and now that he was gone the bulk of the estate would go to Yoko unless she came in to change her will. It was just another case of confronting John's death and it had her in tears.

She was very adamant at the time that since the house would automatically go into John's estate, she wanted Yoko to have nothing else. For some reason she seemed quite concerned about her getting the gold records and awards. She would throw them all into the harbor before Yoko would get them, she told me.

When Mary and I left that afternoon to catch the train to Birmingham, Mimi came out on the terrace to bid us goodbye. She had hugged us both and as I walked away, I turned back to look at her and I knew in an instant that this would be the last time I'd see her.

I was quite sad throughout the long train ride to Birmingham.

Twenty Seven

I never completely understood Mimi's problem with Julian. I do know that the family was always interested in his well-being. There was a time during the very early 70's when Cynthia refused to let John talk to him and one of Mimi's nieces was sent to Cyn's house to find out just what was going on. As I recall the story, it took quite a while for Cynthia to come to the door and the niece was sent on her way rather quickly. But she'd found out that Julian was fine and shortly thereafter he was allowed once again to talk to his father.

I don't believe Mimi ever saw Julian after the divorce. If she did, she didn't mention it. Had she seen him on occasion, I'm sure things might have been entirely different between them. It wasn't until after John's death that a kind of bitterness came through.

All of this is conjecture but I think it might possibly have been the fact that he ran to Yoko first when he had never made any attempt to contact Mimi, then or throughout the years. According to Yoko, she bought him almost anything he wanted and that didn't sit well with Mimi. She felt he was just there for the money, not a terribly endearing character trait. And there was always Cyn. Mimi didn't like her. John didn't like her. Guilt by association for Julian.

It's odd though and in all families there's not always a black or white explanation to any situation.

One of the other girls had been visiting Mimi shortly after I and asked her why she didn't try to get in touch with Julian. She could tell him all about his father and the English half of his family that John had been so keen to do with Sean. Who better?

Mimi began to cry then and said she didn't want to get close to him because Julian already had too much death in his young life. She was old. She didn't want to build a relationship with him and then die on him too.

She apparently didn't have that worry with Sean. She adored him almost from the beginning. He was amazingly intelligent, she said, and she loved talking to him on the phone. I have no reason to believe that adoration didn't continue until she died.

I remember one story she told about Sean. Apparently he had lost his first tooth so Yoko told him to put it under his pillow and the tooth fairy would come and give him money for it. He followed her instructions and came out the next morning, disappointed that he'd received American money. He had hoped for foreign coins. Mimi took that as an early indication of his intelligence and that he would grow up to know exactly how to handle money.

Twenty Eight

I spent the following week in Birmingham; going to a wedding, doing some local shopping, and going to Wales for a couple days in hopes of taking a boat across the Irish Sea to Ireland. We were able to sleep on the boat and I can still remember waking up that morning and seeing the sun highlighting beautiful Conwy Castle in the distance. Unfortunately by the time everyone was up and ready for our excursion the fog had moved in and it was decided it was too dangerous to try and cross that morning. Instead we returned to Birmingham.

Though our trip was cut short, I did like Wales. It seemed amazing to me that as soon as we crossed into that country, the terrain changed completely. Gone were the flat green meadows of England and instead we were circling a mountain on a small road, where goats and sheep grazed unfazed on the side of the mountain.

We arrived in the very small town of Conwy and spent a little time trying to find Lindsay's brother and his girlfriend. They were the ones with the boat. Deciding we were the first to arrive, it seemed the only solution was wait for them in a nearby pub. And so we did.

We occupied our time with drinking, hiding an occasional salt shaker or ashtray or glass in our bags to use on the boat, and even watching a troop of Welsh traditional dancers dancing outside the pub door. It really was a good time.

I had an English sheep dog sitting near me on a bench as if waiting for his own libation. I looked around to see who he/she might belong to but the dog looked to be on his own for that moment. Hope springs eternal but there was no sign of a McCartney in the vicinity.

Once back in Birmingham, it seemed like there was hardly any time before we had to head back to London and Heathrow. Lindsay drove a small mini back, loaded down with me, her young daughter Jemma and two weeks' worth of luggage.

We met up with Mary at Heathrow (she had returned to Southampton after the wedding) and then it was simply a case of doing what you have to do before boarding the plane for the long flight back to Minneapolis. I hated to leave, not realizing it would probably be my last visit.

Twenty Nine

I took a couple extra days off work when I got home. I learned about jet lag the hard way after the first trip in 1973, and if I was going to walk around and think like a zombie, I wanted to be at home. After, of course, it gave me a chance to turn in the meager amount left in traveler's cheques. I can remember getting into the elevator at the bank and having absolutely no idea what I was supposed to do next to make the damn thing move. Ahhh jet lag.

*M*imi and I resumed our conversation through letters. There were still the occasional phone calls, but at $1.00 per minute, they weren't very long. Pity she didn't live long enough to benefit from the "free to anywhere in the world" phone systems.

She had been to visit friends in Wimborne after my visit so I hadn't expected to hear from her right away, and it was the first of October before a rather long letter arrived. She started her epistle off by complaining about the cold, rainy weather and how the sea was bashing against the harbor. Midway through the letter she received a phone call from Marie and the subject changed immediately.

Marie had been to Beatlefest in New York. She had phoned me while there to inform me that Cynthia was there selling copies of her art from her first book. I think this might have been the first of several trips to Beatlefest for Cyn. Marie thought I might want to fly in to meet her, but funds were extremely limited after the trip to England. She did, however, keep me informed of what was going on in that little corner of the 'fest by phone several times a day.

The only thing I remember is she called to tell me that she told Cyn that she knew the former president of the Cyn Lennon Beatle Club and did Cyn think she might ever go to Minnesota.

As I recall it, Cyn replied "*Why would I ever go to Minnesota?*" Well, why, indeed. Unless, of course, she wanted to continue to sell copies of old lithographs at $30 a pop.

Needless to say, Mimi didn't take the news well at all. "*[Marie] nearly fell over herself telling me about Cyn selling at a Beatlefest or whatever you call those things. I couldn't believe it! Whatever is she thinking?!!...It's incredible, undignified, and degrading, to me anyway but then I'm not trying to cash in or seeking publicity. If I had been a cast off wife or mistress I think I would have kept quiet and out of sight especially with two husbands still hanging around somewhere. I'd laugh my head off if they decided to cash in as well. Heaven knows there's no knowing what people will do for money. And they have a story as well.........* *Kathy, I'm half sorry for Cyn. I wonder how and what prompted her to leave herself open to criticism and remarks by people. I phoned my sister* and Liela …...*they say she's desperate for notice, and what's more likely looking for another—er—husband over there. That's the most likely place. What do you bet? Altho I hope she won't be so silly. I don't think she can help it. We'll see. She could not have sold all these drawings at the exhibition, or perhaps she did more for the Beatlefest…….I never saw anything arty she ever did, so have no idea…."*

And from her next letter dated 26 October '81 she continued on in the same vein:

"I was sorry to hear Cyn was renting a table to sell things. How could she do such a thing! Joining that jamboree. It's bound to cause some unfavorable comments. As to why, apart from the obvious. Here's the latest rolling in millions and the first, 14 years almost after the divorce, and two further husbands (still about somewhere) renting a table to sell things – I really am sorry she did it. She was a very wealthy woman. I hope she's still got some of it left. It makes one think she's cashing in on the Lennon name for money. Perhaps I'm too old fashioned. Your note may have cheered her up for I can't think she was very happy standing there, money or no money. It makes me cringe……Whatever Cyn may say I think she's lonely and realizes she was a fool……to be photographed with May Pang and I hear staying with her (if it's true) well, it's rock bottom. I hope she made some money to compensate her for what I think was an undignified escapade. Of course it's only my opinion. I may be entirely wrong altogether. Better if I am wrong."

T hough I had been there when her doctor had come by, it wasn't really until I returned home and she began to mention her ailments more and more often that I began to realize that she really wasn't doing well. In one letter she mentioned that Liela had changed her tablets and she was feeling 100% better. She began to spend more time up North where she said they would "fret" over her, and often times she'd write saying she'd just been in hospital or might even write from the hospital. For the time being, though, the letters kept coming.

Thirty

y May of '82 her letters took on a different theme as she began to hear more and more from Yoko.

"I'm hearing a lot from Yoko. I seem to have phone calls nearly every other day. She says she's very busy. No doubt she is but underlying it all I think she's realizing that without her making an effort etc. nobody will bother much. She needs to be noticed and like an old witch I sense loneliness. Seems next Spring Strawberry Fields will be planted. She wanted me to go over for the opening. I can't give a definite answer. The whole thing may come to nothing. She suggested if I like it over there, would I consider living there as that's what John wanted. I think I'm too old to do that. I could have one of the flats in the Dakota..........

"It was Yoko who said Cyn had an agent, which would explain her emergence. Also she said another book to be written about John. I think I'll scream if I have any more of it. Some journalist called and asked her if I would see him. I will not have my name in it if I can help it."

Considering the timing and all, I've always thought that the journalist she wanted nothing to do with was probably Albert Goldman.

And still the fans came.

"Now some man has asked if I'll accept a painting of John outside the house in Woolton. He sent me a slide and I gather he's made a painting from that. It's 4'x3'. But – he wants to deliver it personally. He lives in Devon. What do I do if it's some amateur, primitive, flat and nothing like him? The slide made me dissolve in tears the whole day. It's him, and very good. I told Yoko about it and she's sending someone down for it. She's going to have an enlargement made of it. I couldn't say no. She's also sending honey for my health. I know it's good. So…I'm getting to know nearly all the office staff she and John employed. Can't think what for but they're there, all right."

In June, I received another letter and the painting had arrived.

"Did I tell you about the painter fan from Devon asking me to accept a painting he had done of John outside the house in Woolton? Well it came. He wanted to deliver it personally but I said I was going North (but not when). It's 4'x3', too big to hang on the wall which he asked me to do. The painting of John is very good. He went to Woolton, photographed the house, which has changed, colours, one thing & another but NOT our house as we had it. He has super imposed John on that as tho leaving the house. It's smiling profile and really very good. He phoned to see if I liked it and I'm worn out telling him how pleased I am and how clever he is, etc. etc.….Where upon he wants to do one of me.….no damn fear! I can't look at myself in the flesh, certainly don't want it in paint.

"Yesterday morning I had all doors open – fatal – a Schoolmaster appeared in a gorgeous new MG Sports Car, a real beauty. He is 35, an avid fan of John's. I offered the usual tea and biscuits. He kept saying "I can't believe I'm talking to Mimi after reading so much and in John's house!" He had spent the whole morning knocking on doors – looking for the house. [He] even went to the Information Desk in Bournemouth and the girl told him it was by the Ferry. He's an English teacher in a

school in Yorkshire. Went to L'Pool University. Even the girl fans have nothing on him. He knew every move John ever made & by the time he left – eventually – I could hardly believe it. I'm always so damned ready to offer a cup of tea when they look so tired after making the effort to find me. I do it automatically. It means nothing, but I'll have to change. I couldn't be caught like that again for hours & hours, never ending. They must think I'm barmy. I think so myself sometimes.

"*By the way, the painting of John when he was about 23, young & handsome. And – life like. It's too much. I've put it away.*"

*T*t was May 1982 and the Falkland War was on the horizon. The talk turned political.

"*I think of the young men in army, navy, and air force, in grave danger. I cried as I watched the ships leaving Southampton. Marines are still practicing in the Harbour and at the army depot in Poole. If things are not settled, they too will go. Heartbreaking….*

"*Don't mention that 1 cent B actor Reagan to me. A great country like USA electing him! He doesn't know from one day to another what he's saying. Recently he said Argentina had a point in their favor. Dictators! With a point! Sooner you get rid of him and his inane wife the better. Don't forget, however minor disagreements US and this country may have, we are your greatest friends. Forgive the outburst…..*"

But it was her outbursts that were always the most interesting if not entertaining.

Thirty One

As the eighties continued, it became more and more apparent that Mimi was not doing well at all, and was in and out of hospital a majority of the time. When I had visited, she joked about the doctor wanting her to give up smoking and it wasn't too long after that she complained of heart problems, without specifically saying what was wrong.

In February of 1983 I received a letter from her from an Arrow Park hospital in Wirral, Liverpool. *"I am in hospital, a private ward. I was not getting stronger and I'm seeing a specialist. Seems I now have a leaking valve in the heart and I'll always have to take things slowly."*

Once released from the hospital, she stayed for quite a few months with her sister, Anne, in Rock Ferry. We would talk on the phone when she was strong enough and letters would arrive periodically.

Her February '84 letter brought about some news. *"Perhaps you heard of Yoko's visit? She came here with Sean, and – dear*

God – body guards! Incredible in this country! She had announced she was coming to see me, so of course the damned press were here from 8 a.m. asking to see me, but I refused. They were persistent, knocking and asking for me but I stuck it out and refused. Meanwhile they sat at the door and waited. What was annoying, they got the address and nobody knew where I was until then. Then the retinue arrived and photographs – of Yoko and Sean.

"Sean – the dearest little boy. Another John in every way – self-confident and sophisticated, taking photographs with timing on the camera and his arms around me. Left me a little letter with kisses and hearts and 'God bless Mimi'. I simply could not get over him. We were all taken with him.

"With Yoko also was a woman reporter, didn't say so until she came and sat beside me and asked why I refused to see reporters. I said because they are all liars, then she said 'I'm on a magazine'....So, if she writes she won't have anything pleasant to say about me. When she got back to NY she phoned and didn't seem very pleased when I said I still had nothing to say. So that was short and sharp. Her name was Barbara. I didn't get the surname. So look out for her article if you can. She was with Yoko everywhere. Came over and went back with her. And – the body guards – dear God –"

Mimi truly adored Sean, and by the mid-80's was warming considerably toward Yoko.

I mentioned how I thought it a bit odd that she would bring a reporter with her when she was coming to see her dead husband's family for the first time since his death, but she merely shrugged it off. *"She can't help herself."*

The Guitar's All Right as a Hobby, John

oward the end of the 80's, her letters were becoming fewer and far between. She seemed to spend more and more time in hospital or rehabilitation centers.

I received my last letter from her in 1987. It was just a few lines. She had fallen and chipped a bone in her shoulder so she was in a nursing home in Charminster, an area in Bournemouth. I received two or three Christmas cards in the years that followed, but we had no further communication as such.

I instinctively knew she was not up to writing or even coming to the telephone any longer, though I continued writing for a while simply to let her know I'd not forgotten her and to keep her abreast of some of the news I thought she'd be interested in.

was at work in December of 1991 when I heard on the radio that she had passed away. Even though the news was inevitable, it shook me to the core at first. There were very few details about Mimi. It was really about the three remaining Beatles each sending a floral arrangement for her funeral and I couldn't help but smile at that. Mimi would have said something critical, I'm sure. You should send flowers to the living so they can appreciate them, not when they've died. But underneath it all I knew she would have been secretly pleased.

By all accounts, she had a rather large memorial service. Yoko and Sean, Cynthia, and I'm sure a great number of the family. The bungalow in Poole would be sold and the new owners announcing that they were demolishing the house and building something more modern. That beautiful little house by the sea would be no more.

Hearing that, I couldn't help but wonder what happened to everything in the house. She had told me after one of her hospital stays that the family had been quite sure that she wasn't going to make it and had gone in and taken a few items. All of John's letters were missing and she wasn't at all sure where they had gone. And I wondered about all the beloved gold records.

I had an e-mail exchange with one of Julian's assistants in the mid-90's when the subject of the gold records came up. The assistant assured me that Julian had certainly not received any. I figured as much since Jules was buying a lot of Beatle gold records at auctions for his own collection. Pity he didn't receive the ones Mimi had. They were all Beatles, no solo gold, and it sounded as if they were just the items Julian was paying for.

Thirty Two

I miss hearing from her immensely. And even today I'll think about how she might have reacted to the different headlines that have occurred since her death. So much has happened since then.

I'm sure she would have had genuine sympathy for Paul after Linda's death, and would no doubt have softened her opinion of Linda as well. Yet I can see her shaking her head in total consternation when Heather Mills made the scene. And God only knows what she would have had to say about their very public divorce.

Despite her dislike of his accent many years ago, George's death would have touched her as well. As would the death of her favorite of all the Beatle People, Derek Taylor.

The deaths of Princess Diana and the Queen Mother would have saddened her. The only Royals she thought worth their weight were the Queen, the Queen Mother and Diana. I'd be afraid to hear what she thought of Camilla, but I'd want to.

September 11th, the Bush wars, the Obama presidency, the terrorists, the Sandy Hook shootings, the July 7th bombings in London and on and on.

So many things had happened that I would have loved Mimi's input on.

⌒

*A*fter Mimi died, I read in several books that her last words were about being frightened of dying because she had been so mean. I suppose it's possible she was afraid, but confessing to being so mean almost sounds like wishful thinking on someone else's part.

A year or so ago, I came across a short passage on the Internet from one of her live-in nurses. Maybe it's wishful thinking on my part this time, but I found it far more believable.

The nurse said Mimi was lying in bed after having collapsed, and her last words were, "*Hello, John*"

I couldn't help but smile at that. I can't imagine she would have wanted anyone else to greet her. Or that he wouldn't have been there. Finally.

Paul was right. She really was a fun character.

Kathy Burns still lives in a suburb of
Minneapolis and is still a Beatles fan.

No animals were harmed in the writing of this book.

Made in the USA
Charleston, SC
11 August 2014